SHARED FOUNDATIONS

Inquire

SHARED FOUNDATIONS SERIES

SHARED FOUNDATIONS

Inquire

LORI E. DONOVAN

CHICAGO | 2020

American Association
of School Librarians
TRANSFORMING LEARNING

Extensive effort has gone into ensuring the reliability of the information in this book; however, the publisher makes no warranty, express or implied, with respect to the material contained herein.

ISBNs
978-0-8389-1916-3 (paper)
978-0-8389-1948-4 (PDF)
978-0-8389-1947-7 (ePub)
978-0-8389-1949-1 (Kindle)

Library of Congress Cataloging-in-Publication Data

Names: Donovan, Lori E., author.
Title: Inquire / Lori E. Donovan.
Description: Chicago : ALA Editions, 2020. | Series: Shared foundations series ; I | Includes bibliographical references and index. | Summary: "Working on the foundation of Inquire and the domains of Think, Create, Share, and Grow, this book will cover how inquiry aids in lifelong learning for the Learner and the Librarian, and how it creates a strong Library program. Working from the theoretical - why inquiry is important for all learners to cultivate and to embrace critical thinking skills, communication skills, collaboration skills, and creativity skills - to the practical application of those skills through the use of inquiry-based research models and activities. This book will also include no-tech, low-tech, and high-tech examples of how to incorporate Inquire into the Learner, Librarian, and School Libraries Competencies so that readers can use/adapt/remix and document student growth"— Provided by publisher.
Identifiers: LCCN 2019027011 (print) | LCCN 2019027012 (ebook) | ISBN 9780838919163 (paperback) | ISBN 9780838919477 (epub) | ISBN 9780838919484 (pdf) | ISBN 9780838919491 (kindle edition)
Subjects: LCSH: School libraries—Aims and objectives—United States. | School librarian participation in curriculum planning—United States. | Inquiry-based learning. | Libraries and schools—United States.
Classification: LCC Z675.S3 D67 2019 (print) | LCC Z675.S3 (ebook) | DDC 027.8—dc23
LC record available at https://lccn.loc.gov/2019027011
LC ebook record available at https://lccn.loc.gov/2019027012

♾ This paper meets the requirements of ANSI/NISO Z39.48-1992 (Permanence of Paper).

Printed in the United States of America
24 23 22 21 20   5 4 3 2 1

Purchases of AASL Publications fund advocacy, leadership, professional development, and standards initiatives for school librarians nationally.

ALA Editions purchases fund advocacy, awareness, and accreditation programs for library professionals worldwide.

SHARED FOUNDATION I
Inquire

Build new knowledge by inquiring, thinking critically, identifying problems, and developing strategies for solving problems.

Contents

Acknowledgments

This book would not be complete without my acknowledgment of the following groups of people who went along for the ride and without whom this book would not be possible. My sincerest appreciation to:

- AASL for this opportunity to write about one of my passions—inquiry learning.
- My school division's learners, school librarians, and educator partners for sharing their time and expertise to make this book possible.
- My library colleagues and friends who submitted lessons for the chapters on the Domains.
- My family for their patience with all the notes on the kitchen wall as I organized my thoughts to outline this book's development, and all the times I was shut away in the bedroom writing and phone conferencing.

Series Introduction

The Shared Foundations series from the American Association of School Librarians (AASL) examines the six Shared Foundations that anchor the comprehensive approach to teaching and learning in the *National School Library Standards for Learners, School Librarians, and School Libraries.* The Shared Foundations—Inquire, Include, Collaborate, Curate, Explore, and Engage—represent the core concepts that all learners, school librarians, and school libraries develop and promote in their K–12 learning environment.

Each of the six books in this series is dedicated to the deep exploration of a single Shared Foundation. Although each of the Shared Foundations supports its own inherent priorities, it cannot be implemented in isolation. The writing process used by the authors created a series of books that, like the AASL Standards Frameworks, are unique and yet parallel each other. Common elements are found throughout the series:

- A balance between theoretical discussion, practical strategies, and implementation examples, promoting reflection and creativity
- Development of the Competencies and Alignments for the Learner, School Librarian, and School Library in all four Domains—Think, Create, Share, and Grow
- Differences in application and assessment across grades K–12, promoting a growth mindset and envisioning outcomes for all learners, whether student learners, school librarians, or other educators
- An emphasis on personalized learning experiences, project-based learning, and authenticity of learning and projects
- Challenges addressed, illustrating ways to implement the Shared Foundations in various environments and levels of support

Questions for the Reflective Practitioner conclude each chapter, allowing readers to consider the application of concepts specific to their own learning communities and stimulate nuanced professional conversations. For ease of reference, readers also will find the AASL Standards Integrated Framework for the relevant Shared Foundation included in this work.

AASL and its series authors hope that this immersive and dedicated examination of the Shared Foundations will help school library professionals deepen their understandings, broaden their perspectives, make connections for personal relevance, and innovate and reflect on their practice with a professional community.

For more information about the *National School Library Standards,* and to access the latest implementation assistance resources, visit standards.aasl.org.

Inquire

Domain	LEARNER DOMAINS AND COMPETENCIES	SCHOOL LIBRARIAN DOMAINS AND COMPETENCIES
A. Think	**Learners display curiosity and initiative by:** 1. Formulating questions about a personal interest or a curricular topic. 2. Recalling prior and background knowledge as context for new meaning.	**School librarians teach learners to display curiosity and initiative when seeking information by:** 1. Encouraging learners to formulate questions about a personal interest or a curricular topic. 2. Activating learners' prior and background knowledge as context for constructing new meaning.
B. Create	**Learners engage with new knowledge by following a process that includes:** 1. Using evidence to investigate questions. 2. Devising and implementing a plan to fill knowledge gaps. 3. Generating products that illustrate learning.	**School librarians promote new knowledge generation by:** 1. Ensuring that learners probe possible answers to questions. 2. Devising and implementing a plan to fill knowledge gaps. 3. Facilitating the development of products that illustrate learning.
C. Share	**Learners adapt, communicate, and exchange learning products with others in a cycle that includes:** 1. Interacting with content presented by others. 2. Providing constructive feedback. 3. Acting on feedback to improve. 4. Sharing products with an authentic audience.	**School librarians guide learners to maintain focus throughout the inquiry process by:** 1. Assisting in assessing the inquiry-based research process. 2. Providing opportunities for learners to share learning products and reflect on the learning process with others.
D. Grow	**Learners participate in an ongoing inquiry-based process by:** 1. Continually seeking knowledge. 2. Engaging in sustained inquiry. 3. Enacting new understanding through real-world connections. 4. Using reflection to guide informed decisions.	**School librarians implement and model an inquiry-based process by:** 1. Leading learners and staff through the research process. 2. Constructing tasks focused on learners' individual areas of interest. 3. Enabling learners to seek knowledge, create new knowledge, and make real-world connections for lifelong learning.

KEY COMMITMENT

Build new knowledge by inquiring, thinking
critically, identifying problems, and
developing strategies for solving problems.

SCHOOL LIBRARY DOMAINS AND ALIGNMENTS	The school library facilitates the Key Commitment to and Competencies of INQUIRE	Domain
	The school library enables curiosity and initiative by: 1. Embedding the inquiry process within grade bands and within disciplines. 2. Using a systematic instructional-development and information-search process in working with other educators to improve integration of the process into curriculum.	**A. Think**
	The school library enables generation of new knowledge by: 1. Providing experiences with and access to resources, information, ideas, and technology for all learners in the school community. 2. Supporting flexible scheduling to provide learner and educator access to staff and resources at the point of need.	**B. Create**
	The school library provides learners opportunities to maintain focus throughout the inquiry process by: 1. Creating and maintaining a teaching and learning environment that is inviting, safe, adaptable, and conducive to learning. 2. Enabling equitable physical and intellectual access by providing barrier-free, universally designed environments. 3. Engaging with measurable learner outcomes and with data sources to improve resources, instruction, and services.	**C. Share**
	The school library ensures an inquiry-based process for learners by: 1. Establishing and supporting a learning environment that builds critical-thinking and inquiry dispositions for all learners. 2. Reinforcing the role of the school library, information, and technology resources in maximizing learning and institutional effectiveness.	**D. Grow**

Preface

I have always been interested in learning more, solving puzzles, reading mysteries. I played school growing up. My family does jigsaw puzzles together. My husband and I complete the newspaper's crossword puzzles after dinner. I have read mysteries my whole life, from *Encyclopedia Brown* to *Nancy Drew* and *Trixie Belden,* and even now love to curl up with a mystery and a cup of tea. The inquiry process draws me in. Even as an educator, I have always been after the "why." Why does an author use this language or this motif to tell her story? Why does the language an author chooses allow the reader to dive into the story? Why do some learners catch on to things that take other learners more time?

Curriculum and instruction are my strong points. The many different ways to approach learning fascinate me. When I read about a new writing or literacy strategy, I always tried it out in my classroom. I let my learners know that the activity was an experiment to see if a particular strategy really worked (or not). If I learned something at a library conference, I always knew which educator partners I would share it with first, which ones were the most open to trying something new–even if it bombed. When I began my school librarianship degree, the inquiry process that is such a foundational part of learning really clicked with me. Looking at and studying different inquiry models and working with learners to develop critical and creative thinking skills were amazing, eye-opening revelations to me.

Modeling lifelong learning through an inquiry process has always been a part of my journey in my education career. Moving from the English classroom to the school library was a natural progression in my own inquiry as well as in my educational journey. Deepening my research on the pedagogy of inquiry led me to helping other school librarians help their learners master the inquiry process skills needed to contribute as critical and creative thinkers in a global society, which in turn led me to writing this book. I am excited to share my thinking and research as well as practical approaches that school librarians and other educators can use to develop a culture of inquiry in their own communities.

To learn means by practice, by inquiring, by analyzing
to find out what is, not what was.

—Lobsang Tenzin

Introduction:
Finding a Path to Inquire

Inquiry is the foundation of all learning. As humans, we all wonder who, what, why, and how about our world. It is this curiosity that creates critical-thinking skills within learners. Asking questions like "What if . . . ?", "I wonder . . . ?", and "How would this look if . . . ?" allows learners to dive deep into topics that interest them and to know more about their world. School librarians foster this curiosity through deliberate and intentional lessons in the school library, introducing inquiry processes through reading literacy, information literacy, digital literacy, and media literacy. Curious, transliterate learners become curious adults who are able to think critically, tinker, and create innovative solutions to problems.

As you read this book, you will walk through the Shared Foundation of Inquire from AASL's *National School Library Standards for Learners, School Librarians, and School Libraries*. By connecting current research related to inquiry-based learning with teaching practices and inquiry models, you'll begin to build your own strategies for developing competent inquirers and inquiry cultures to support lifelong learning. Working through the lens of the Shared Foundation of Inquire and framed by each of the Domains—Think, Create, Share, and Grow—you will read theoretical and applicable practices relating to the Competencies and Alignments for learners, school librarians, and school libraries. Within each Domain, examples of inquiry-based learning are featured, as well as no-tech, low-tech, or high-tech strategies and applications, so that no matter the school or school library, all learners can develop inquiry skills. For the purpose of this book, no-tech tools are defined as traditional teaching tools; low-tech tools are easy, online tools that can be used independently or collaboratively in a single setting; and high-tech tools are tools that can be used at any time during the inquiry process or used over a course of time. Many high-tech tools are subscription based or have a licensing fee attached. Be sure to review your district's policy for purchasing and using technology tools before using them with educators and learners.

Last, although this book's focus is on the Shared Foundation of Inquire, we'll conclude by examining how Inquire connects with the other Shared Foundations—Include, Collaborate, Curate, Explore, and Engage. By exploring their interconnectedness, we'll consider how these other five Shared Foundations also depend on learners' ability to identify and negotiate questions, making Inquire truly a bedrock of our Shared Foundations.

This book is designed to help school librarians understand the science and research behind inquiry learning as it relates to the *National School Library Standards*. I hope this understanding enables you to customize your approach when implementing the Shared Foundation of Inquire with learners and other educators. I hope that in this book you will find practical applications to lessons that foster inquiry and that allow you to visualize and build a school culture that harnesses that curiosity.

PART I

Framing Inquire

1

Defining Inquiry

Humans are naturally curious creatures. Through inquiry, learners discover how generating their own questions about personal or curricular topics aids the inquiry research process. Learner-generated questions build deeper understanding and better retention of the topic studied. Learners who use questioning techniques begin to understand that different types of questions bring different answers, that questions have purpose, and that through practice, learners develop the capacity to ask higher order thinking questions. Learners also learn that when they ask their own questions, the new learning tends to become embedded with prior knowledge because those questions were developed through their own curiosity about the topic.

Warren Berger stated in *A More Beautiful Question: The Power of Inquiry to Spark Breakthrough Ideas,* "Among those who've studied the needs of the evolving workplace from an educational standpoint the consensus seems to be that this new world demands citizens who are self-learners; who are creative and resourceful; who can adjust and adapt to constant change" (Berger 2016, 49).

The school library is an ideal setting to engage learners to become resourceful and adaptive citizens. The *National School Library Standards* Shared Foundation of Inquire sets learners and classroom educators on the path to cultivating this type of citizenry through its Competencies and Alignments. Under the direction and supervision of a certified school librarian, learners learn how to ask good questions and devise plans for answering those questions facilitated through the school library space and information and technology resources.

What Does It Mean to Inquire?

"Although individuals may not always consciously reflect on their inquiry processes, the process of asking questions, gathering information, making sense of the information, making decisions, and sharing results is something we all do every day" (AASL 2018, 28). Inquiry is internal; it is innate. Children begin to understand their surroundings and environments through inquiry. Once children are able to speak, questions are formed. Young children know they don't know, so they ask questions—and "an efficient way to fill the gap in their knowledge [is] by asking someone who might know" (Berger 2016, 41).

WHO SHOULD BE DOING THE INQUIRING?

Most educators use the Socratic method of teaching—the educator asks questions, learners ponder the questions and possible answers, and then learners answer the questions. The Socratic method works well when educators need to know what learners do and do not know. But this method doesn't help create learners who know how to inquire themselves; they only know how to answer someone else's questions.

"Many educators acknowledge it's critically important that students be able to formulate and ask good questions . . . and realize that this skill is apt to be more important in the future, as complexity increases and change accelerates. Yet, for some reason, questioning isn't taught in most schools—nor is it rewarded" (Berger 2016, 2). If that is the case, it is all the more imperative that school libraries and school librarians take up the mantle of teaching learners how to ask questions—not only how to formulate them but also how to work through developing and answering those questions themselves.

Teaching learners the ability to ask the *right* question is key. Berger has studied hundreds of successful people and has found that those who are the most successful know how to ask the right questions and know how to locate answers to those questions. The AASL *National School Library Standards* moves the learner forward with an integrated framework for the Shared Foundation of Inquire (see pages xii–xiii of this book) that includes a Key Commitment, Domains, and Competencies, providing school librarians and other stakeholders a process by which learners can develop the necessary skills to navigate this increasingly complex, global world.

WHEN SHOULD INQUIRY HAPPEN?

Learners are not often enough given a chance to ask questions. They are asked to *answer* a lot of questions, though. What is missing is the opportunity for learners to understand why we ask questions, what a good question looks like, how good questions are formed, and how to work through solving or finding answers or possible solutions to questions. Being able to ask a good question is a learned skill. In today's fast-paced world, technology can answer a question in fractions of a second, but how to teach good questioning and the time needed to teach good questioning are often in conflict.

Dan Rothstein and Luz Santana of the Right Question Institute have studied this phenomenon. Using the *Newsweek* study on the "Nation's Report Card" in 2009, they found that young children ask lots and lots of questions, but from the time these same children start school to the time they graduate, the amount of questions they ask diminishes by 75 percent. Rothstein and Santana noted a decline in engagement as learners progress through school as well: from 76 percent engaged in elementary school to 61 percent in middle school and to 44 percent in high school (Berger 2016, 44–45).

If schools and school libraries are to develop learners who become citizens who are motivated and creative problem solvers, then the teaching of inquiry skills needs to happen at all grade levels, in all content areas, and as often as possible. The framework for Inquire guides school librarians in lesson development with classroom and content-area educators and reveals opportunities to document learners' growth and engagement. It is critical that school librarians document and promote strong instructional partnerships, demonstrating the role school libraries play in facilitating and cultivating an inquiry culture at all grade levels.

WHERE DOES INQUIRY HAPPEN?

Opportunities for inquiry can happen anywhere, but all library work starts with Inquire, whether looking for a new book to read, answering a research question for personal or academic pursuits, or exploring and innovating new ideas. The basis of Inquire is knowing how to ask good questions and find answers. School librarians can foster this skill by

- stopping at certain points during a read-aloud to ask questions and model active listening and reading;
- helping learners discern their personal likes and dislikes in what they want to read;
- beginning any inquiry project by modeling questioning techniques, such as the Question Formulation Technique, Essential Questions, Fishbowl activities, and the like; and
- creating a makerspace in the school library where learners can explore, design, test, reflect, and solve problems using resources within the space.

HOW DOES INQUIRY HAPPEN?

School librarians foster a culture of inquiry by partnering with other educators to collaboratively plan, design, and deliver instruction. "Inquiry requires students to engage in active learning by generating their own driving questions, seeking out answers, and exploring complex problems" (Holland 2017). Berger stated that "students must develop the 'habit' of learning and questioning, that knowledge cannot be force-fed to them" (Berger 2016, 53). For some learners and educators, this approach will be a huge shift. In the age of high-stakes testing in which funding, evaluations, tenure, and even jobs are on the line, moving from "force-fed" knowledge dumping to an inquiry-based model, and allowing the time for this process to develop, requires an institutional shift. This shift means that school librarians need to provide opportunities for all learners—students, educators, and administrators—to design occasions to inquire. But don't think inquiry-based learning units have to start from scratch or be pounded into the content curriculum to make them fit. Most, if not all, of the core content areas have inquiry built into their professional standards. Opportunities abound to make standards and curriculum connections and to start conversations with potential educator partners.

On an episode entitled "Should Educators Design Google-Proof Questions?" on NPR's *All Tech Considered,* Zhai Yun Tan stated that for "millennials and post-millennials, Google and Siri are regular 'go-tos' for answers. While this is great for simple questions that provide simple, easy responses, this is not good if educators are looking to foster inquiry and then use critical-thinking skills to demonstrate new understandings about the curricular content." For example, Tan related a story about an educator who wanted his learners to dive deep into the research question by deciding what resources they needed, how to evaluate the information found within those resources, and how to reconcile different points of view. What really happened was that learners Googled the research question word for word (Tan 2016). School librarians and their educator partners need to collaborate so that the inquiry part of the learning unit is designed with a very specific purpose. The inquiry part needs to lead learners through the process of critical and creative thinking in order to solve a problem or answer a research question.

One of the best ways to build learners' competency in Inquire is by using an inquiry-based research process model when designing unit lessons. Daniel Callison and Katie Baker discussed the five elements of information inquiry and inquiry models. They noted that no matter what inquiry process model is being used, all the models start with questioning. "Questions trigger the interactions that can eventually lead to greater understanding of an environment, a situation, a problem, an issue, or actions of a person or group" (Callison and Baker 2014, 18). Whether educator created or learner created—though research shows that learners are more engaged and have better work output if they create their own questions—all inquiry needs to start with the definition of *inquire:* "to ask about; to search into" (https://www .merriam-webster.com/dictionary/inquire). In order for learners to develop questioning skills, inquiry-based learning needs to follow a specific processing path that is supported by the Learner Competencies.

The best inquiry process models use a constructivist approach because it allows learners to build upon their foundational prior knowledge as well as their foundation of new knowledge and to make new meaning and connections in learning. If learners are to learn how to best frame inquiry, methods must be in place to support and sustain that development. The school librarian and the classroom or content-area educator work collaboratively to combine content learning and information literacy, engaging learners to make connections from prior knowledge to new knowledge.

WHY SHOULD INQUIRY SCAFFOLD?

Using an inquiry-based learning model helps learners navigate through the process of inquiry. Using scaffolds throughout the process, school librarians and their educator partners lead the learners to develop the critical-thinking skills necessary to participate in an ever-changing global society.

"Well, my teachers leave the research teaching up to me, and I [the school librarian] really don't have a say in what the research project *could be*." Is teaching research the same as teaching inquiry? No. "Research, though often a component of inquiry, addresses the process of finding answers. . . . While research can certainly exist as a stand-alone process, inquiry should ultimately drive students to view research as a means through which they can seek out new ideas, answer new questions, and wrestle with complex problems" (Holland 2017). Most research projects that learners come to the school library with fall into what David Loertscher and colleagues described as "bird units," or prepackaged, regurgitated assignments that do not actually engage learners with an inquiry process (Loertscher, Koechlin, and Zwaan 2005). Using an inquiry process model that focuses on questions and questioning techniques is important not only for teaching the critical-thinking skills necessary for participation in a global society but also for engaging the learner with the learning of the content and information literacy skills.

Creating Lifelong Learners

The *National School Library Standards* Shared Foundation of Inquire pulls together the research about questioning and how the inquiry process plays a role in the development of critical thinkers and creative lifelong learners. As our world grows more complex, it is more important than ever for learners to become competent inquirers who display initiative through pursuing personal interests and curiosities. Learners who can employ an inquiry process to solve problems will begin to see authentic purposes for their questions, becoming more resourceful and adaptive citizens. To question the world around us is instinctive, but developing the skills for good question formulation must be taught, early and often. Building competent inquirers is an exercise in repetition as learners grow in an expanding and ever-changing global world. Through the Shared Foundation of Inquire, school librarians and their educator partners have a roadmap to use when setting goals and expectations for learners, collaboratively designing and delivering instruction that guides learners through an inquiry process fostering question generation and answer finding. The time required to engage in deep, scaffolded inquiry processes may be an instructional shift for both learners and educators. But documenting and sharing examples of learners' growth through successful instructional partnerships will go a long way toward cultivating an inquiry culture in the school library that will eventually permeate learning communities throughout the school.

Questions for the Reflective Practitioner

1. What can I do to foster a culture of inquiry and encourage inquiry learner–developed questioning across all content areas and grade levels?

2. How can I work with other educators to design an inquiry unit that truly taps into the skills learners need to develop for work beyond a K–12 school environment?

3. What content curriculum connections can I make with the Competencies in the Shared Foundation of Inquire, and how can I use those connections to get the conversation started?

2

Understanding Process and Questioning

School librarians like to think of the Shared Foundation of Inquire and the inquiry process as a detective game. Playing Sherlock Holmes to find the right resource for the right person at the exact time that person needs it is the fun part of being a school librarian. Inquiry learning process models help learners walk through an inquiry unit much like a detective. Each process has a series of steps or clues that move the detective (learner) forward so that a conclusion or hypothesis can be reached.

The goal of any inquiry learning unit is to have learners use their prior knowledge about a personal interest or curricular topic and apply new knowledge to demonstrate the critical- and creative-thinking skills needed to showcase new learning. Inquiry learning process models guide learners as they work through a series of questions generated by the learner. School librarians and their educator partners facilitate guided lessons on using those questions to develop hypothesis or thesis statements and draw a conclusion using data found during the inquiry process.

Using an inquiry process model and questioning techniques sets learners on a path that allows them to make connections between prior knowledge and new knowledge gained during this process. The Learner Competencies for Inquire integrate well with many inquiry-based process models, and these Competencies provide opportunities to document evidence of learners' growth in content curriculum and information literacy skills.

9

Process Models Supporting Inquire

There are quite a few inquiry process models that school librarians and their educator partners can use to help facilitate inquiry learning. The following inquiry process models are not the only methods but are four of the most commonly used process models in school libraries. These four models were specifically chosen because they synchronize well with the Domains and Competencies of the Shared Foundation of Inquire in the *National School Library Standards*.

Each of the four process models described includes steps, stages, or phases of inquiry learning that help school librarians and other educators design instruction that supports the learner's journey through the Shared Foundation of Inquire and the Domains of Think, Create, Share, and Grow. In later chapters, these models and processes are explored more deeply in practice relative to each of the Domains and through lesson examples.

GUIDED INQUIRY DESIGN

Developed by Carol C. Kuhlthau, Leslie K. Maniotes, and Ann K. Caspari, Guided Inquiry Design (GID) enables the cultivation of a collaborative inquiry culture in a school community. GID begins with a learning team that develops an inquiry unit that leads learners to deeper understanding of core content and information literacy skills (Kuhlthau, Maniotes, and Caspari 2015, 3–4). GID takes learners through a framework that aids in the design not only of instruction but also of a learner's model for "how to learn." The GID model involves eight phases—Open, Immerse, Explore, Identify, Gather, Create, Share, and Evaluate—that naturally unfold across time. Although linear-looking, these phases overlap in a series of connected learning experiences, much like the Domains in the AASL Standards. While following the phases of the GID model, learners will jump back and forth between Think and Create, sometimes simultaneously exercising Inquire Competencies in these Domains before moving on to Share and Grow (figure 2.1).

BIG6

Developed by Mike Eisenberg and Bob Berkowitz, the Big6 model "integrates information search and use skills along with technology tools in a systematic process to find, use, apply, and evaluate information for specific needs and tasks" (Big6, n.d.). This six-step process model, with two substages in each step, takes learners through the inquiry process to solve an information problem. When combined with content curriculum goals, the six steps—Task Definition, Information Seeking Strategies, Location and Access, Use of Information, Synthesis, and Evaluation—help learners of all ages become systemic thinkers as they focus on process as well as product. Eisenberg and Berkowitz state that learners don't need to go through the steps in a linear order. Again, like the Inquire Domains, sometimes learners will need to backtrack through the steps when obstacles or changes in direction occur while solving

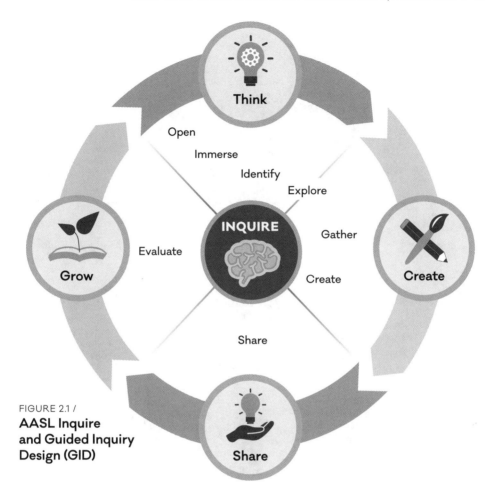

FIGURE 2.1 /
**AASL Inquire
and Guided Inquiry
Design (GID)**

the problem or research question. When following the Big6 process model, a blurring of steps occurs primarily while building learners' Competencies in the Create and Share Domains for Inquire (figure 2.2).

STRIPLING MODEL OF INQUIRY

Developed by former AASL and ALA president Barbara Stripling, this model assists learners through the inquiry process in phases that are recursive and reflective. The Stripling model focuses on the inquiry that learners do when their personal understandings connect to their work. As learners go through the six stages—Connect, Wonder, Investigate, Construct, Express, and Reflect—each learning experience should lead to new knowledge, allowing learners to make connections with prior knowledge and create new understandings. These new understandings lead to new questions and, therefore, new inquiry. This inquiry spiral is echoed in the Shared Foundation of Inquire (figure 2.3). As is particularly emphasized in the Grow Domain, learners are expected to participate, continually seeking and engaging in an ongoing inquiry process guided by reflective decision making.

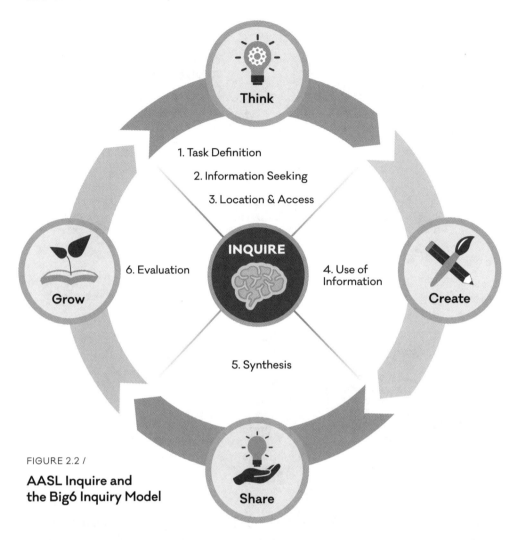

FIGURE 2.2 /

**AASL Inquire and
the Big6 Inquiry Model**

PATHWAYS TO KNOWLEDGE

Developed by Marjorie L. Pappas and Ann E. Tepe, and sponsored by Follett, the Pathways to Knowledge model focuses on the importance of questioning and authentic learning. This nonlinear process is used with learners to help them find, use, and evaluate information. The Pathways process allows learners to explore and reassess information as they move through six stages:

- Appreciation and Enjoyment (examine the world)
- Presearch (develop an overview; explore relationships)
- Search (identify information providers; select information resources; seek relevant information)
- Interpretation (interpret information)
- Communication (apply information; share new knowledge)
- Evaluation (evaluate process and product)

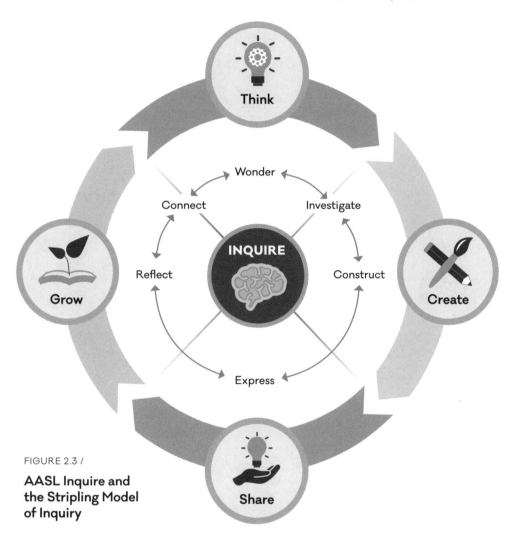

FIGURE 2.3 /

AASL Inquire and the Stripling Model of Inquiry

Similar to the other models described, as learners progress from the Presearch stage through the Communication stage of the Pathways process, developing the Competencies of Inquire may overlap in the Think, Create, and Share Domains. However, the Pathways model also introduces a unique element in which learners may begin with the end. During the Appreciation and Enjoyment stage, learners develop Competencies in both the Grow and Think Domains of Inquire (figure 2.4). By beginning the inquiry process by examining and making connections with the world around them, learners grow an appreciation for subjects and materials. This appreciation can foster curiosity and serve as a prelude to questioning and continued information-seeking activity.

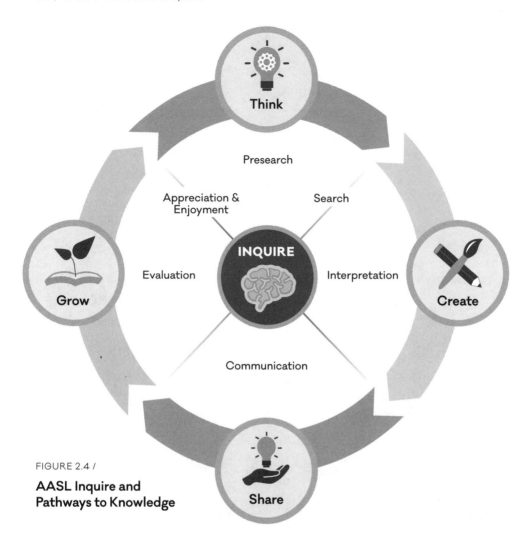

FIGURE 2.4 /

AASL Inquire and Pathways to Knowledge

Questioning Protocols Supporting Inquire

Inquiry process models begin with questioning. School librarians and their educator partners teach learners the importance of questioning at the beginning of the unit, revise and develop more questions as learners narrow their focus, and develop reflective questions to locate gaps in knowledge gathering. At the end of the unit, learners self-reflect on the process as a whole. Questioning techniques or protocols can be used in conjunction with any inquiry process model and help learners identify the difference between inquiry and research. The following examples of questioning protocols were chosen because they are some of the best known and easiest to implement anywhere within the inquiry process. These questioning protocols also pair well with the inquiry process models discussed in this chapter and throughout the book. Last, these questioning protocols provide school librarians and their educator partners with formative and summative evidence to support learner growth in content curriculum and in developing the Competencies of Inquire.

QUESTION FORMULATION TECHNIQUE

The Question Formulation Technique (QFT) from the Right Question Institute is a step-by-step process that easily works into any part of the inquiry process. It is a "process for students to produce questions using a set of four simple rules, improve on their questions, prioritize their questions, plan for next steps and reflect on what they have learned, how they learned it and how they will use what they have learned" (Rothstein and Santana 2011, 4). School librarians and other educators develop a Question Focus (QFocus) that becomes the basis for learners' questions. Question development can be done independently or in a group. Learners follow four simple rules:

1. Ask as many questions as you can.
2. Do not stop to discuss, judge, or answer any of the questions.
3. Write down every question exactly as it was stated.
4. Change any statements into questions.

Learners then talk about open- and closed-ended questions and change one of each type of question in their list before prioritizing the questions. Learners choose three questions to begin their inquiry and justify their choices as they plan how to move forward with those questions. At the end of the activity, learners reflect about the process and the product. This self-reflection provides the learners time to use convergent, divergent, and metacognitive thinking skills in one activity.

By taking learners through a "rigorous process in which they think more deeply about their questions, refine them, and prioritize their use," learners learn how to harness their natural curiosity and develop divergent thinking, convergent thinking, and metacognitive thinking (Rothstein and Santana 2011, 4). The QFT takes learners through a process to aid in the building of new knowledge by inquiring, asking questions, thinking critically, and categorizing and prioritizing questions, highlighting major points in the Key Commitment of Inquire.

When beginning the QFT process, make sure to model it with learners. At the beginning of a unit of study that supports science or history and social studies, having learners pose questions related to a chart, graph, map, or image can help frame learners' inquiry and move it in the direction the educator wants the lesson to go. Educators direct learners through the development of the QFocus. A QFocus "has a clear focus; is not a question; provokes and stimulates new lines of thinking; and does not reveal educator preferences or bias" (Rothstein and Santana 2011, 29). The QFocus is the setup to invite learners into the inquiry process model guiding the learning unit.

WHY? WHAT IF? HOW?

In *A More Beautiful Question,* Berger introduced the "Why, What If, and How of Innovative Questioning" as an easy problem-solving process that takes learners through a three-step system leading to a possible solution. Berger described the process this way: "Person encounters a situation that is less than ideal; asks *Why*. Person begins to come up with ideas for possible improvements/solutions—with such ideas usually surfacing in the form of *What If* possibilities. [Then] person takes one of those possibilities and tries to implement it or make it real; this mostly involves figuring out *How*" (Berger 2016, 32; italics added).

The Why? What if? How? process brings in the four components of creativity: preparation, incubation, illumination, and implementation. The Why? stage is important because Berger's research pointed out that nonexperts or outsiders are better at asking questions than are insiders or experts. *Why* is about the seeing and understanding, the knowing that something is wrong or broken or just not working. The What If? stage really hones in on the creative- and critical-thinking parts of problem solving. And the How? stage is about the doing. This protocol is a great way to integrate questioning and problem solving with service learning and problem- or project-based learning activities.

Berger's process replicates the idea of design thinking to systematically solve problems or make improvements to ideas and processes that need fixing. A similar progression—from understanding a problem to imagining possible solutions to then going to work on those possibilities—can also be seen in the creative problem-solving process (Berger 2016, 32–33). The Why? What If? How? process provides an easy way to teach questioning and "an attempt to bring at least some semblance of order to a questioning process that is, by its nature, chaotic and unpredictable" (Berger 2016, 33). For learners who are beginning a questioning process, Why? What If? How? is one questioning protocol that can frame what inquiry process models could look like. The Why? What If? How? protocol can also be done quickly, allowing learners to find some measure of success, especially learners who don't often find success in their learning.

ESSENTIAL QUESTIONS

In *Understanding by Design,* Wiggins and McTighe argued that Essential Questions are the basis for keeping learners on track with the big ideas they will be learning in a content class. "They serve as a doorway through which students explore key concepts, themes, theories, issues and problems that reside within the content, perhaps as yet unseen. It is through the process of actively 'interrogating' the content through provocative questions that students deepen their understanding" (Wiggins and McTighe 2005, 106). Wiggins and McTighe laid out four connotations that an Essential Question must have: help learners see that questions occur all the time and for every subject; point to the core of what needs to be known; help learners learn how to ask the right questions in order to find an answer; and engage learners to *want* to know the answer (Wiggins and McTighe 2005, 108–109). Essential Questions can help learners gain competency in the Inquire Think Domain because Essential Questions are a model for learners to develop their own questions about the content to be learned.

NEED TO KNOW LIST

The Buck Institute for Education's Project Based Learning (PBL) model uses a Need to Know List that helps make learner inquiry visible. Questions are crafted about what learners need to know about an inquiry unit. These questions guide learners as they create products that demonstrate their learning. A Need to Know List is a physical list in the classroom or school library of what learners feel they need to know in order to answer the Driving Question, much like the Essential Question described in *Understanding by Design*. Having learners develop a Need to Know List allows the school librarian and educator partner to guide learners through an ongoing inquiry-based process.

"If we want learners to develop questioning skills, [then the Need to Know List] is a process to coach them with multiple opportunities to shape their queries. . . . Such questions can raise engagement by learners as they search for answers, which oftentimes lead to deeper and more complex questions" (McCarthy 2016). Referring often to the Need to Know List during the lesson or unit, and revisiting the question set as needed, demonstrates to learners the importance of "continually seeking knowledge" throughout the inquiry process, developing competency in the Grow Domain of Inquire (AASL 2018, Learner I.D.1.). Lessons that frame and scaffold learning allow learners to grow their dispositions and competency for "engaging in sustained inquiry" (AASL 2018, Learner I.D.2.).

SEE, THINK, WONDER

The See, Think, Wonder routine, one of the Core Routines from Visible Thinking and Harvard Project Zero, encourages learners "to make careful observations and thoughtful interpretations. It helps stimulate curiosity and sets the stage for inquiry" (Harvard Project Zero, n.d.a). See, Think, Wonder can be used at the beginning, middle, or end of a unit to help engage learners with objects that make connections to the learning skills in the inquiry unit. The routine works like this:

- Begin by asking learners to make an observation about an object, artwork, image, artifact, or topic.
- Follow up by asking learners what they think might be going on or what they think this observation means. Encourage learners to back up their interpretation with evidence or reasons.
- Finally, ask learners what their observations and interpretations make them wonder about the object or topic.

The routine works best when a learner responds by using the three stems together at the same time—that is, "I see . . . , I think . . . , I wonder . . ." (Harvard Project Zero, n.d.a). However, with younger learners, begin with one stem at a time and then scaffold each response with a follow-up question for the next stem. I like to use this routine in professional development with school librarians and classroom educators. See, Think, Wonder is also a great routine to model engagement with primary sources for learners.

HOW MIGHT WE

As part of design thinking, "How Might We questions are a way to frame . . . ideation, and [are] often used for launching brainstorms. . . . The goal is to create questions that provoke meaningful and relevant ideas; do so by keeping the questions insightful and nuanced" ("How Might We" Questions, 2019). As part of the Design Process model, the How Might We protocol allows educators to help learners frame a problem-solving challenge, especially for STEAM (science, technology, engineering, the arts, and mathematics) or PBL units, from many different points of view. This structured protocol is a helpful practice for critical and creative thinking and is particularly useful for school librarians who have a makerspace where learners can tinker.

5 WHYS METHOD

The purpose of the 5 Whys protocol is to get at the foundational root of a question and to uncover multiple perspectives on the question. According to the School Reform Initiative, the protocol works like this:

- An educator will pose a question to the learners and describe the context of the question. Learners can respond with a few questions to further clarify the context.
- The group then brainstorms potential answers to the initial "why" question.
- The group chooses one of those answers to become a new "why" question, taking the group deeper into the inquiry
- The group repeats this question-answer-question brainstorm cycle for a maximum of five rounds. The educator should silently observe throughout the process.
- Finally, the group discusses potential answers to the last "why" question surfaced, before debriefing the experience together and with the educator (School Reform Initiative, n.d.).

The brainstorm and discussion that unfold are not attempts to solve a problem; rather, they are attempts to understand the underlying cause of the issue in question. Through the discussion, learners may also identify relationships between multiple root causes to the given problem. Getting to the root cause may take fewer or more rounds than the five "why" questions. Asking the right questions is critical to uncovering the right answer. A question that is asked in the right way often points to its own answer. The 5 Whys protocol is most useful when the resolution involves human factors or interactions. This protocol is useful with a student advisory team when thinking about change in the school library, classroom, or community. This protocol is also useful for reflecting on learning or content during a grade-level or subject-area professional learning community or personal learning network meeting.

Aligning Inquiry Structures

The inquiry process models and questioning protocols described in this chapter provide an overview of the popular structures and techniques that school librarians and other educators can use to guide inquiry-based learning experiences. Questioning techniques can be used at any point in the inquiry process and blend well with the inquiry process models represented. When used in combination, these tools can help school librarians and other educators design dynamic inquiry-based lessons and units related to curricular topics that also build learner Competencies in the Shared Foundation of Inquire. Applications of the Domains in learning are not always linear, nor are the phases expressed through the inquiry models, but they lead learners through a process, allowing them to practice questioning, locating, accessing, and using information from a variety of sources. Through the inquiry process, learners will also discover that specific sources offer certain types of information that other sources cannot, helping learners discern bias and contradictory statements as they create learning products for an intended audience.

These process models and questioning protocols also provide opportunities for school librarians to document evidence of learners' competence and growth in the Domains as well as in learners' understanding of curricular content. More-specific discussion of these processes and techniques and how they relate to each of the Domains for instructional purposes, along with instructional examples, is found in the following parts and chapters.

Questions for the Reflective Practitioner

1 In what ways can I use inquiry process models to build a culture of inquiry in and beyond the school library?

2 In what ways can I incorporate questioning techniques into my existing inquiry lessons to help build learners' critical- and creative-thinking skills?

3 How can I engage with other educators about process models and questioning techniques to create partnerships and collaboratively plan, design, and deliver dynamic inquiry-learning units?

3

Applying
Appreciative Inquiry

If you were thinking about creating more innovation in the school library, where would you start? Perhaps you would think of all the past times when the library was the spark of innovation at the school. Alternatively, you might think about what a truly innovative school library would look like—how would the materials, methods, and space need to change? Then you might work to create a vision that is invigorating and inspiring. Once your vision is clear, you would likely identify the steps needed to reach that vision. Perhaps you might create models and prototypes, map steps, identify needed resources, and engage the support of others. Then you would work to make your vision a reality. If you followed these steps, you would be engaging in Appreciative Inquiry.

What Is Appreciative Inquiry?

Whitney and Trosten-Bloom, in *The Power of Appreciative Inquiry: A Practical Guide to Positive Change,* define Appreciative Inquiry (AI) as an "approach to personal change and organization change . . . based on the assumption that questions and dialogue about strengths, successes, values, hopes, and dreams are themselves transformational. In short, Appreciative Inquiry suggests that human organizing and change, at its best, is a relational process of inquiry, . . . grounded in affirmation and appreciation" (Whitney and Trosten-Bloom 2010, 1). Appreciative Inquiry began in the business world to bring about institutional change. "At its heart, AI is about the search for the best in people, their organizations, and the strengths-filled, opportunity-rich world around them. . . . AI is a fundamental shift in the overall

21

perspective taken throughout the entire change process to 'see' the wholeness of the human system and to 'inquire' into that system's strengths, possibilities, and successes" (AI Commons, n.d.b.).

Since its introduction, AI has been adopted by many educators and used for organizational or instructional improvement, as well as with learners as a research method in inquiry learning. AI stresses the importance of ensuring that all voices are engaged and heard during the inquiry process, emphasizing the strengths of the learner and uncovering the best of what is, what could be, what should be, and what will be regarding the learner's topic of research. This positive approach relies on the belief that people nurture what they appreciate, amplifying and motivating learners' success by reinforcing relationships and culture, promoting learning and innovation, and inspiring action.

Learners, as they work through an inquiry process, focus on what is working to help them develop new knowledge to answer their research question or prove their hypothesis. In doing so, AI allows learners to persevere when faced with challenges, and their ultimate success encourages transferable learning skills and dispositions. AI can do the same for educators when they assume the role of learner during strategic planning, professional development, or collaborative instructional planning and can influence inquiry culture across the school community.

Moving Beyond the Default

Brain researchers talk about how the brain compartmentalizes learning. The brain learns when to conceptualize the input it receives from short-term memory to long-term memory. Every day, rote work often repeated becomes so automatic that it doesn't require active thought to bring it forward from memory. Maura O'Neill, the chief innovation officer for USAID, said, "We make judgement about what's 'known' based on everything we've experienced already . . . the more we see, hear, touch, or smell something, the more hardwired in our brain it becomes. We routinely default to the set of knowledge and experience each one of us has" (Berger 2016, 79). School librarians can help build a learner's catalog of hardwired memories or rote work by designing learning experiences with and providing access to a variety of resources, information, ideas, and technology.

O'Neill's illustration of learning builds upon that ability to recall memory and apply new knowledge to that memory so that the learning will "stick." In *A More Beautiful Question* Berger stated that O'Neill's premise works for most circumstances, "but when we wish to move beyond that default setting—to consider new ideas and possibilities, to break from habitual thinking and expand upon our existing knowledge—it helps if we can let go of what we know, just temporarily" (Berger 2016, 79). School librarians and their educator partners need to collaborate to design the types of learning experiences that celebrate the fact that no one knows everything, and that is okay; that is why learners are doing what they are doing. Appreciating that unknown element leaves room for new ideas and innovations.

Appreciating the Unknown

Inquiry involves "asking about" or "searching into." True inquiry requires learners to step back from knowing. "The act of inquiry requires sincere curiosity and openness to new possibilities, new directions, and new understanding. We cannot 'have all the answers,' 'know what is right,' or 'be certain' when we engage in inquiry" (Whitney and Trosten-Bloom 2010, 3).

Berger's research showed why successful people succeed: they know and accept that they don't know and are comfortable with that ignorance as well as understand the context of questions and questioning (Berger 2016, 78). This acceptance and understanding are skills that must be taught and fostered. No better place than the school library.

To build this inquiry learning in a positive, affective way, learning must happen in a safe environment in which failing forward is a teachable moment as opposed to a stopgap that some learners feel when learning something new is a struggle. Learners need to be comfortable with not knowing, and the culture surrounding the learning environment needs to support that uncomfortableness of not knowing in order for true inquiry to happen. Appreciation places value, ownership, and recognition at its core. For school libraries and school librarians, this appreciation is the learning "space" that is developed: that all learners, educators, and stakeholders feel value and worth; that their contribution to the community is meaningful to them as well as to others. Designing and developing a culture in which learners and educators feel welcome to share thoughts and ideas, to fail forward and fail quickly, and to learn from those failures is important in order to meet the Key Commitment of Inquire.

Enabling Independent Learners

If words create worlds and inquiry creates change, setting up learners to succeed at the beginning of the inquiry learning unit is important. AI stresses that voice and choice are important in order to effect change; for student learners that change is added to their prior knowledge so that learners can show growth in the subject matter content and information literacy skills. Helping learners frame questions to guide their inquiry process empowered by their own curiosity leads to better critical thinking and development of strategies for problem solving.

All four inquiry process models applied in this book employ specific scaffolds for inviting inquiry by learners. Each of these models includes questioning by learners in order to determine the path they will take during the inquiry unit. As learners begin the inquiry process, school librarians and other educators are asked to move into a facilitator role rather than remain as the lead instructor, meaning that most of the direct instruction throughout the inquiry process needs to come from the learners. To do this, school librarians and other educators use systems that will enable learners to develop metacognitive skills as they work through the inquiry unit.

The goal in any lesson planning is to teach skills within one frame of context so that those skills can then be applied at a higher level in another context or subject area. In designing an inquiry unit, it is important to consider the skills and dispositions that learners need to develop in order to independently take their learning to an application or transferrable stage.

Setting the Stage for Appreciative Inquiry

The goal of all learning is that learners not only learn the content being taught but also feel a measure of success while doing so. Developing collaborative lessons that provide the content learning and build information literacy skills while developing the disposition of perseverance is what AI can bring to an inquiry process unit.

When school librarians and their educator partners sit down to plan a collaborative inquiry unit, they too engage as learners in the application of Appreciative Inquiry, focusing on the strengths each educator brings to the table—the school librarian guiding information literacy skills and the educator partner guiding content-area skills. By using each collaborator's strengths, an inquiry unit can be created that will support a positive learning outcome. Collaborative planning at the beginning of a unit is emphasized as being crucial by all inquiry process models.

Outside their individual curriculum goals, to ensure learners' success the school librarian and content educator must think about the learners who will be working through the unit and examine these questions as they plan:

- *What are the strengths and growth areas for the learners as they work through this unit?* Both the school librarian and content educator will look at learner dispositions within the standards that focus on persistence when faced with challenges in the learning process.
- *What types of scaffolding can be in place to build a growth mindset and metacognitive development?* Carol Dweck, Lewis and Virginia Eaton Professor of Psychology at Stanford University, stated, "In a growth mindset, people believe that their most basic abilities can be developed through dedication and hard work—brains and talent are just the starting point. This view creates a love of learning and a resilience that is essential for great accomplishment" (Glossary of Education Reform, 2013). School librarians and classroom educators put in place scaffolds that nurture this growth mindset as learners work through the learning unit, thereby enabling learners to achieve success.

- *What scaffolds will need to be in place so that learners can experience what AI calls the "Positive Principle"?* The Positive Principle is this: "Momentum for small- or large-scale change requires large amounts of positive affect and social bonding" (AI Commons, n.d.a).

In developing a culture of inquiry, school librarians must first endeavor to make the school library a safe, nurturing environment in which learners can experiment and challenge themselves, knowing there is support if they stumble. However, spreading these cultural ideals throughout the school community can easily be amplified when educators collaborate. Through collaborative planning of inquiry units, school librarians can use the concepts of AI to aid in the development of dispositions to persevere despite having to overcome obstacles, so learners achieve success.

Appreciative Inquiry's 4-D Cycle

Appreciative Inquiry works through the 4-D Cycle—Discovery, Dream, Design, and Destiny—with the concept that "individuals, teams, organizations, and communities grow and change in the direction of what they study" (Whitney and Trosten-Bloom 2010, 6).

In some literature, AI involves a fifth stage. The two models are very similar. In the 5-D Cycle, "Define" becomes the first stage and serves to clarify the purpose or topic to be explored. This additional stage perhaps fits better with AI's business model, originally designed to help guide big organizational change. When considering inquiry learning, having the Discovery already defined may take away from learners' voice and choice and limit learners' ability to discover their own path to their learning. For the purposes of this book, the 4-D Cycle (figure 3.1) will be used to demonstrate how school librarians and other educators can work together using AI as they plan inquiry units of study.

Teaching critical thinking requires school librarians and their educator partners to develop and then scaffold learning experiences. Using scaffolds, learners apply their prior knowledge about the content and then apply new knowledge in a way that demonstrates the connection of the two. The 4-D Cycle can be applied to motivate critical thinking during the inquiry process whether solving a problem, creating a new product, proving or disproving a hypothesis, or determining an author's purpose in a novel.

AI's 4-D Cycle has scaffolds built into its process that align well with the Domains of Inquire. However, an appreciative approach to inquiry is a philosophy, not a technique. First, we'll explore the stages of the 4-D Cycle as a philosophy and their alignments with the Shared Foundation of Inquire. Then we'll discuss inquiry models and questioning techniques that can help you initiate the stages of the 4-D Cycle, allowing this approach to influence your culture and community.

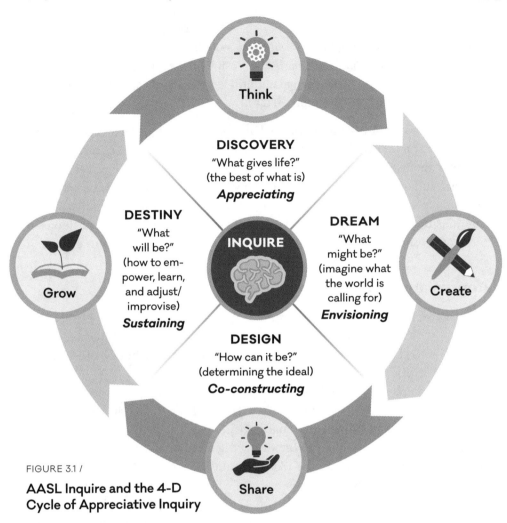

FIGURE 3.1 /

AASL Inquire and the 4-D Cycle of Appreciative Inquiry

DISCOVERY

The 4-D Cycle's Discovery stage is "an extensive, cooperative search to understand the 'best of what is and what has been,'" focusing on knowing what learners already know and what they don't know (Whitney and Trosten-Bloom 2010, 7). This stage in the 4-D Cycle aligns with the Think Domain of Inquire because learners display curiosity and initiative while performing Discovery (table 3.1). Learners formulate questions, using background and prior knowledge to enhance and refine those questions. Sustaining inquiry, learners use new and refined questions to seek new knowledge. Connecting learning to prior knowledge and real-world situations provides context and meaning, allowing learners to *discover* the best of what is or has been and *create* a world of what could be.

Ways to Initiate Discovery

The following questioning protocols require learners to step back from the knowing and open themselves to possibilities:

TABLE 3.1 / **Discovery and the Inquiry Process**

INQUIRE: THINK	Discovery: "What gives life?" Appreciating the best of what is or has been.			
	Guided Inquiry Design	**The Big6**	**Stripling Model of Inquiry**	**Pathways to Knowledge**
	Open: Sets the tone and direction for learning.	*Task Definition:* Learners define the problem.	*Connect:* Use prior knowledge to set context for new meaning.	*Presearch:* Make connections between topic and prior knowledge (what learners know and want to know).

- QFT: List "discovered" questions that learners have prioritized as wanting to know more about or what needs to be learned first in order to move on in the inquiry process.
- Need to Know: Using the PBL model, create a Need to Know List based on the Driving Question.
- Why? What If? How?: Change something, fix something, or solve a problem.

DREAM

The 4-D Cycle's Dream stage is "an energizing exploration of 'what might be.' It is a time to envision possibilities that are big, bold, and beyond the boundaries of what has been in the past" (Whitney and Trosten-Bloom 2010, 8). The Dream stage aligns with the Create Domain of Inquire because learners engage with their new knowledge. In this stage, learners will begin to add to their prior knowledge, see conflicts within the learning, and use critical-thinking skills to decide how to move forward or backward or both by using multiple resources to fill knowledge gaps (table 3.2). The Dream stage encourages learners to keep seeking knowledge as they reflect on their work, adding context to new learning and building a vision.

Ways to Initiate Dream

Once learners have determined the direction of their inquiry, they are ready to move into the Dream stage of the cycle, devising a plan to fill knowledge gaps and illustrate their vision.

- Build background knowledge with the information that is available, and determine what information is needed from the Discovery stage.
- Use a robust print and online collection as well as other resources.
- QFT: Work through learner-identified priority questions.
- Why? What If? How?: Move into the What If? stage to plan out how to solve the problem or issue.

TABLE 3.2 / **Dream and the Inquiry Process**

Dream: "What might be?"			
Imagining what the world is calling for and envisioning results.			
Guided Inquiry Design	**The Big6**	**Stripling Model of Inquiry**	**Pathways to Knowledge**
Immerse: Connect with the content to discover interesting ideas to explore further. *Explore:* Review all possible resources that could aid in the inquiry process and create research question(s).	*Information-Seeking Strategies:* Determine all the possible sources of information that might answer learners' questions. *Location and Access:* Drill down into the information and prioritize the most important information that will move learners' task definition forward.	*Wonder:* Develop questions and make predictions or hypotheses.	*Search:* Identify appropriate information providers, resources, and tools, then plan and implement a search strategy to find information relevant to the research question or information need.

(Left margin label: INQUIRE: CREATE)

DESIGN

The 4-D Cycle's Design stage is "a set of Provocative Propositions, which are statements describing the ideal, or 'what should be'" (Whitney and Trosten-Bloom 2010, 8). In the Design stage, learners decide where their learning is going to go. Aligning with the Share Domain of Inquire, the Design stage allows learners to adapt, communicate, and exchange learning products with others and to interact with content presented by others (table 3.3). Through cycles of giving, receiving, and reflecting on feedback, learners improve upon and co-construct their expressed dreams or visions.

Ways to Initiate Design

School librarians can help facilitate learning in the Design stage through scaffolded learning experiences, including micro lessons on how to evaluate materials and identify resources that are most likely to answer learners' research questions and prove or disprove their hypotheses.

- QFT: Refine and prioritize questions based on new information gained during resource evaluation.
- Use inquiry logs and other graphic organizers to organize, prioritize, or throw out information that is not relevant to the inquiry process.

TABLE 3.3 / **Design and the Inquiry Process**

<table>
<tr><td rowspan="2"></td><td colspan="4">Design: "How can it be?"
Determining and co-constructing the ideal.</td></tr>
<tr><td>Guided Inquiry Design</td><td>The Big6</td><td>Stripling Model of Inquiry</td><td>Pathways to Knowledge</td></tr>
<tr><td>INQUIRE: SHARE</td><td>Identify: Construct an inquiry question for the interesting ideas, pressing problems, and emerging themes learners have explored in various sources of information.

Gather: Go broad and go deep for understandings of learners' resource questions and make connections to personal learning.</td><td>Use of Information: Engage with multiple resources to move the learner's task definition forward.</td><td>Investigate: Find, evaluate, and use information to create new questions and move a hypothesis forward.</td><td>Information: Process of analyzing, synthesizing, and evaluating information to determine its relevance and usefulness to the learner's research question or information need.</td></tr>
</table>

- Peer review can help learners identify gaps, determine bias, or point out discrepancies within the context of gathering and synthesizing knowledge.

DESTINY

The 4-D Cycle's Destiny stage is "a series of inspired actions that support ongoing learning and innovation, or 'what will be'" (Whitney and Trosten-Bloom 2010, 9). Through connecting to the Grow Domain of Inquire, learners will be inspired to participate in ongoing inquiry-based processes. As learners share products with an authentic audience, they develop new understandings through making real-world connections (table 3.4). All the inquiry process models stress the need to reflect not only on the product demonstrating the new learning but also on the process by which the learning took place, so learners have an opportunity to build metacognitive skills. Learners become inspired to engage in sustained inquiry, empowered to consider how they may adjust or improvise in the future.

Ways to Initiate Destiny

Strengthening and affirming learners' capabilities are key to the Destiny stage. Creating opportunities throughout the learning for learners to build hope and sustain momentum with their abilities and contributions builds a foundation of appreciation.

TABLE 3.4 / **Destiny and the Inquiry Process**

INQUIRE: GROW	Destiny: "What will be?" How to empower, learn, and adjust or improvise and sustain.			
	Guided Inquiry Design	**The Big6**	**Stripling Model of Inquiry**	**Pathways to Knowledge**
	Create and Share: Guide learners to reflect on all they have learned about their inquiry question, construct their own understanding, and decide what type of presentation to do to showcase new knowledge. *Evaluate:* The learning team evaluates how well the learners moved through the inquiry process and mastered the learning goals as well as guides the learners through the self-assessment process after the learning experience is done.	*Synthesis:* Learners put all their information together to show how the information task was solved or the research question was answered. *Evaluation:* Learners then evaluate the process and the product.	*Construct:* Construct new understandings connected to previous knowledge; draw conclusions about questions and hypotheses. *Express:* Express new ideas to share learning with others and apply understandings to a new context or situation. *Reflect:* Self-reflect on learners' own process of learning and on new understandings gained from inquiry and ask new questions.	*Communication:* Organize, apply, and present new knowledge relevant to the learner's research question or information need. *Evaluation:* Evaluate the process of learning and make revisions when and where information searching was wrong or a struggle. Learners also need to evaluate the product to make sure they have correctly communicated the application of new knowledge.

- Use tools (journals, logs, and charts) provided by various inquiry models to help learners document learning and reflect throughout the inquiry process.
- Conference with learners at specific moments to determine whether content learning and metacognitive development are moving in the direction of new learning and application of knowledge with real-world connections.

Why Appreciative Inquiry Works

According to Whitney and Trosten-Bloom, AI works because "it treats people like people, not machines. As humans, we are social. We create our identities and our knowledge in relation to one another. We are curious. We like to tell stories and listen to stories. . . . We like to learn and use what we learn to achieve our best. . . . Appreciative Inquiry works because it liberates power" (2010, 18–19). The authors then state the six reasons why AI works:

- AI builds relationships, enabling people to be known in relationship rather than in a role.
- AI creates opportunity for people to be heard.
- AI generates opportunities for people to dream and to share their dreams.
- AI creates an environment in which people are able to choose how they contribute.
- AI gives people both discretion and support to act.
- AI encourages and enables people to be positive. (Whitney and Trosten-Bloom 2010, 19–20)

Through AI, school librarians can bring about a culture shift, "establishing and supporting a learning environment that builds critical-thinking and inquiry dispositions for all learners" (AASL 2018, School Library I.D.1.). AI encourages other educators to see the school librarian as a valued partner and helps reinforce "the role of the school library, information, and technology resources in maximizing learning and institutional effectiveness" (AASL 2018, School Library I.D.2.).

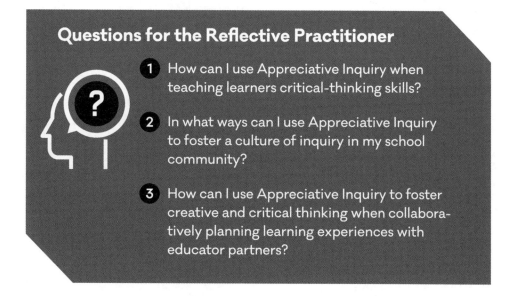

Questions for the Reflective Practitioner

1. How can I use Appreciative Inquiry when teaching learners critical-thinking skills?

2. In what ways can I use Appreciative Inquiry to foster a culture of inquiry in my school community?

3. How can I use Appreciative Inquiry to foster creative and critical thinking when collaboratively planning learning experiences with educator partners?

PART II

Think

4

Moving from Inquiring to Learning

The Inquire Think Domain can open many doors for learners. For a learner looking at the economic causes of a war, using primary sources from that period and looking for a pattern of causality will be that learner's door to deeper understanding of the past. To understand how photosynthesis impacts the amounts of oxygen and carbon dioxide that are absorbed and released, creating a hypothesis and then following the scientific method to prove or negate the hypothesis is the door to understanding and the path to creating new knowledge. When studying how literature is a product of its time, reading several books of that time to look for common themes and motifs is this learner's doorway. Like the many entry points for puzzles, what door a learner goes through to enter the inquiry process should be rooted in curiosity and initiative.

The Inquire Think Domain Competencies are not just part of research, PBL, or formal types of learning. Developing these Competencies teaches learners how to be active readers and speakers as well as how they best learn, adapt, and improve in their metacognitive development. To best support learners as they develop critical-thinking skills, school librarians need to collaboratively plan inquiry units that not only meet the Competencies but also promote curiosity and initiative.

Formulating Questions

To help learners understand that good questions are acceptable and encouraged, educators must develop a culture of inquiry through teaching and modeling question generation skills. When school librarians model questioning for a variety of purposes, learners gain background about the types of questions being asked and determine the purpose for which they will be answered.

School librarians and educators can establish the inquiry culture right at the start of the school year. Establishing class norms and structures for how questions will be handled sets the stage for learners' acceptance that questioning teaches them about perspectives that may be different from their own. The Kagan Cooperative Learning method has approaches for developing a caring classroom community. "Classbuilding provides mutual support among all the students in a class and creates a positive context for learning" (Kagan and Kagan 2015, 9.1). Classbuilding creates an environment in which learners feel valued and safe so that they will be able to engage with the content, feel free to ask questions, fail forward, and have the disposition to move on despite the failure.

When modeling questioning during content instruction, frame questions that include a positive supposition to encourage a growth mindset ("When we last talked about this, you may have made connections to . . ."), include critical- and creative-thinking verbs to model that thinking, and always make sure to allow think time for learners to process the question asked (Lloyd 2015). The following questioning protocols aid in developing learners' competencies when "formulating questions about a personal interest or a curricular topic" (AASL 2018, Learner I.A.1.).

QFT

Using the QFT, learners can ask relevant questions about the previous day's work or upcoming work, generate questions to use as guides for reading, and identify specific topics for research, essays, experiments, and PBL assignments. Learner questions can be used to assess prior knowledge, identify gaps in information and understanding, and shape or refine lesson plans for the next day or for entire units. Through questioning, learners can also shape their own action steps for moving forward and can discover gaps in their learning.

As learners finish their inquiry process, asking questions relevant to just-concluded work, either as self-reflection or as part of peer evaluation, helps learners prepare final reports, presentations, and other products to illustrate learning. Questions developed in this stage also allow school librarians and other educators to assess how well learners moved through the process, evolving their question development from beginning to end.

The QFT has been used with school librarians as part of their professional development. Using a QFocus helps school librarians define their learning for the session. Unanswered questions are then used to develop extensions or new professional development opportunities in the future. In addition, the QFT can help school librarians as learners to develop their own questions to engage with a personal or curricular topic.

ESSENTIAL QUESTIONS

Essential Questions are a good way for school librarians to model what good questions should look like. For educators who are developing questions for learners to use as a model, Wiggins and McTighe discussed the differences between topical and overarching Essential Questions. Topical questions are specific to understandings that need to be gained during the course of the unit. Overarching questions take learners beyond the topic to general but transferable skills that can be used across content areas and units of study. Wiggins and McTighe cautioned that educators need not get caught up in the language of the questions. "If our true intent is inquiry, it will be reflected in what we ask students to do (or not) with the questions" (Wiggins and McTighe 2005, 114). The authors went on to say that there should be enough Essential Questions within a unit so that learners can uncover the main ideas, skills, and understandings learners need to learn. The following are examples of Essential Questions in two content areas.

> *Life Science:* All learners will apply an understanding of cells to the functioning of multicellular organisms, including how cells grow, develop, and reproduce (Michigan State Standards).
> - *Topical Essential Questions:* How can we prove that cells make up living things? If we're all made up of cells, why don't we look alike?
> - *Overarching Essential Question:* How do scientists prove things?

> *Dance:* Understanding dance as a way to create and communicate meaning (National Standards for Arts Education).
> - *Topical Essential Questions:* What ideas can we express through dance? How can motion convey emotion?
> - *Overarching Essential Questions:* In what ways do artists express what they think and feel? In what ways does the medium influence the message? What can the artist do that the non-artist cannot? (Wiggins and McTighe 2005, 119)

Essential Questions are a great exercise when collaborating with educator partners. Using Essential Questions, school librarians and other educators can determine the learning goal that needs to be met by the learners, helping learners see context for the content learning. Through this process school librarians can also work with learners to develop supporting questions that guide learners to the answer to the Essential Question.

NEED TO KNOW LIST

The Need to Know protocol is an important exercise done at the start of a PBL unit. This process is a great formative assessment for identifying what learners know (or do not know) about the upcoming unit. "After the end in mind is shared, including the major product, performance, or other final assessment, students generate questions about what they need to know about the unit so that they can complete the final artifacts, and all tasks that build towards the culminating event or experience" (McCarthy 2016). The Need to Know protocol involves two phases.

Phase 1: Providing learners an appropriate amount of time for reflection and questioning and a structure that honors collaboration is critical before sharing out with the larger group. Combining Need to Know with the Think-Pair-Share protocol is one way to create equity of voice in the inquiry process. Each group then shares questions to develop a class list of questions. The school librarian may ask clarifying questions, but "should not stop to answer, add or direct learners with questions in this process so as not to take ownership away from the learners" (McCarthy 2016). Using a Need to Know protocol with information literacy lessons also provides school librarians an easy way to assess what parts of a learning unit will need to be refined or reinforced through additional coaching opportunities.

Phase 2: Continue referring to the Driving Question throughout the PBL unit. When learners understand the content but struggle to make connections to the project, reviewing the Need to Know List of questions frequently helps learners see the connection. The list serves as a formative assessment check by learners and educators for a common level of understanding (McCarthy 2016).

HOW MIGHT WE

Working through the Design Process model, learners begin by identifying a need or problem, such as how to make a barge like those the ancient Egyptians used that will float on water. As learners work through developing questions about what materials would be needed or the size of the vessel, learners begin to research barges in ancient Egypt, develop prototypes, test, and rebuild (if necessary). The questions at the beginning of the Design Process set learners' thinking in motion.

5 WHYS METHOD

The 5 Whys protocol is good to use in short inquiry projects, helping to direct learners to the learning objective. To guide learners in discovering the answers needed to meet the learning target, educators will need to be very specific in developing the initial question from which learners build their 5 Whys questions. Examples of initial questions used with the 5 Whys protocol could include these: "Why does the poet use this literary element here to create mood or tone in the poem?" "Why does the composer choose to change tempo at this point in the composition?" "Why do we celebrate the Fourth of July?"

These questioning protocols help learners see that the types of questions asked have purpose and that the answers they find give meaning to the question, either to create understanding or to create more questions. As school librarians work with other educators to develop learning units, using a variety of questioning protocols helps to engage learners' curiosity and initiative, enabling them to connect new learning to prior knowledge.

Prior Knowledge as Context

"Learners who harness their prior knowledge to bring new meaning to the answers to their questions take a first step toward addressing their knowledge gaps, building collective knowledge, and strengthening intellectual tools to sustain an inquiry process" (AASL 2018, 28). Connecting new learning to past learning provides context and allows learners to engage in critical and creative thinking as they create new meaning during an inquiry process. Learning to collaborate and to communicate that learning allows transference of skills and knowledge to other content and units.

It is important to construct a supportive learning environment when working with learners to "[recall] prior and background knowledge as context for new meaning" (AASL 2018, Learner, I.A.2.). Providing such an environment allows learners to feel comfortable in not "knowing all" and in the idea that not every solution works. When learning doesn't go the way learners expect, learners need to have the disposition to carry on, knowing that the school librarian has in place supports to see them through the learning process. In a "safe, accepting learning environment in which questions are welcomed and encouraged, learners are empowered to display curiosity and build on prior and collective knowledge in new ways that bring meaning and background to their questions" (AASL 2018, 70). The following strategies demonstrate supports that school librarians can incorporate in inquiry units to help learners build on their background knowledge to gain new knowledge.

K-W-L CHART

The K-W-L (Know, Want to Know, Learned) chart process focuses on what learners *know,* what they *want* to know, and what they *learned* in an inquiry unit. "Using a K-W-L chart, students can prepare to research a topic and use it to track information gathered along the way. This tool will help students confirm what they know about a topic and encourage them to think about how they want to focus their research" (ReadWriteThink 2019). The chart can also be used as a formative assessment, and school librarians can build scaffolds throughout the journey to help learners address learning gaps and build on collective knowledge through a collaborative process.

5 WHYS METHOD

The 5 Whys method naturally builds on the learners' prior knowledge. It asks learners to use collective knowledge to ask the clarifying questions needed to then frame the focus on inquiry that will lead the learners through the inquiry process. In addition to helping learners understand that question forming has a purpose, the 5 Whys method can help learners identify gaps in learning. Using the 5 Whys method, learners can focus on a piece of what their fellow learners are demonstrating and use "why" questions to get to the root of what is missing or not clear. Questions become about the "what," not the "who," taking the sting away from peer feedback. Questions by peers can help learners hone in on those gaps by looking at the "why."

THINKING MAPS

One of the most often used means for helping learners think through a process is a graphic organizer. Thinking Maps are specific types of graphic organizers that help learners make connections to learning by identifying patterns and connections ("What Are Thinking Maps?" n.d.). Thinking Maps provide learners a visual representation of their thinking by creating concrete images of thought and serve as a formative assessment to help guide learners through the learning unit. Thinking Maps are tools that school librarians can use to engage learners' curiosity and initiative. Once learners are engaged with the content through questioning protocols, they can begin making connections and bringing context to prior knowledge and new learning.

School librarians can also use Thinking Maps when developing five-year plans in a district setting. Using a visual peak, school librarians can envision small, easy changes, midrange outcomes, and long-term outcomes and then engage in reflection and introspection, again making adjustments. Modeling differentiated inquire stances when leading district planning or professional development allows school librarians to expand their own toolboxes with protocols that can work for their own learners.

Driving Curiosity

As learners' practice questioning, school librarians can incorporate more tools, demonstrating for learners that questioning and well-formulated questions have a purpose when seeking new knowledge for personal and academic pursuits. Learners need to know not only how to ask good questions but also what resources to use to answer those questions and bring context to their learning, making connections to prior knowledge. However, engagement is key, and the learner's own curiosity and initiative must set the agenda and drive the inquiry process for learning to endure and transfer to other content or units. Collaboratively planning units that use protocols as the vehicle for questioning allows the learner to take the wheel under safe and supported conditions.

Questions for the Reflective Practitioner

1 How can I use questioning protocols to aid in fostering learners' curiosity during an inquiry unit?

2 How can I partner with content-area educators to develop inquiry units that engage learners in using prior or background knowledge to make new meaning?

3 Which strategies might be most effective in helping me promote curiosity and initiative in learners who struggle most to engage with content being studied?

5

Modeling Inquiry

t is lunchtime in the crowded faculty lounge. Educators are sitting around planning, grading, talking with their professional learning community teams while eating their lunches. Listening in the back is the school librarian, who happened to stop in for a coffee and restroom break. The school librarian overhears a professional learning community team going over the latest development marker tests, worried about how to move learners forward. Other educators are attempting to jazz up a unit in which learners seem to be bored with the learning process. It is here where the school librarian can identify potential partnerships and gather ideas to help other educators design inquiry units that address these concerns.

School librarians partner with other educators to collaboratively design scaffolded learning opportunities in which both educators model active thinking and reflecting as learners move through the inquiry unit. "The school librarian captures learner interest with intellectually rich, appropriate, and rigorous ideas, and nurtures questioning behaviors" (AASL 2018, 71). This approach takes time to plan, and there are often circumstances beyond the school librarian's control (weather, testing, etc.). However, learners still need to feel that they are safe and in a well-organized learning environment. In addition to making available content-rich print and digital resources, school librarians can help their educator partners by teaching inquiry-based skills that support questioning, allowing the other educators to focus on guiding learners within the content learning objectives.

Formulating Questions

"The school librarian facilitates collaborative work groups in which multiple viewpoints and ideas are included in the inquiry process" (AASL 2018, 71) by using research-based techniques to teach learners with emphasis on the 4 Cs —critical thinking, creativity, collaboration, and communication. These techniques, when employed, inspire curiosity and initiative while "encouraging learners to formulate questions about a personal interest or a curricular topic" (AASL 2018, School Librarian I.A.1.). School librarians can mentor their educator partners in the value of educator-to-educator and learner-to-learner collaborations, enabling learning outcomes to be met in a more-timely manner with two minds working together. All learners become more engaged with content and learning if paired with like-minded learners.

The following inquiry process models use collaboration as part of question development, question refinement, and question answering. Developing learners' ability to communicate, collaborate, and use critical- and creative-thinking skills builds capacity as learners learn from each other and grow to recognize learning in a social context.

GUIDED INQUIRY DESIGN

Third Space theory, often using virtual tools, merges what learners bring with them to the learning situation with the content-learning outcomes of the unit. Guided Inquiry Design (GID) has scaffolds built into the process through the use of Inquiry Circles, which can take on several formats. Learners can look at the same source and analyze it from different angles, or learners can look at different sources and identify commonalities among the sources to help synthesize information. Educators need to design these units to include various methods and options for communicating to ensure that all learners can feel a part of the learning community. Inquiry Circles can utilize technology, allowing learners to collaborate while in the school library or outside school with online collaborative applications. In order for this framework to be successful, a safe and accepting environment must be in place. Inquiry Circles can be used to review many sources through a jigsaw activity, before learner groups come together to share what was discovered. This method encourages learners to ask even more questions, building their inquiry logs of possible sources. Working collaboratively with inquiry logs can also facilitate work that requires learners to synthesize, prioritize, and even justify uses of sources in order to answer their research question.

BIG6

The Big6 framework provides learners a set of milestones to attain along their inquiry journey, even though they may have to go back a step or stay on a step longer than they did the previous one. As learners work collaboratively to make connections and to formulate opinions and hypotheses, they begin to see patterns that require critical and creative thinking in order to answer their questions. The six stages incorporate supports and resources to guide collaborative thinking with learners. The Big6 website shares a resource for educators to use for evaluation, and *Evaluating Big6 Units* by Barbara Jansen (2004) helps ensure that during the development of the inquiry unit, opportunities are built in for collaboration among learners.

STRIPLING MODEL OF INQUIRY

In the Wonder and Investigate stages of the Stripling model, opportunities for collaboration are plentiful. Using peer questions, learners can wonder about different points of view when deciding which resources to use. Using anticipation guides or graphic organizers, or both, learners can demonstrate through visible thinking what conclusions they are beginning to draw, leading to more questions that set up the Investigate stage. As in GID and Big6, using technology tools to collaborate with other learners creates an environment of trust to move the inquiry process along. Visual representations are a way to differentiate questioning and then, depending on the type of graphic organizer used during this stage, help learners begin to or continue to make connections between prior learning and new learning.

PATHWAYS TO KNOWLEDGE

All stages in the Pathways to Knowledge process model allow for learners to work collaboratively, but most especially in the Interpretation stage. In the Interpretation stage, the synthesis of the inquiry process is honed as learners begin making new meaning from what they knew and what they now know. Many of the specific strategies referenced include critical- and creative-thinking tools that can be implemented with or without technology, such as drawing conclusions, filtering for bias, comparing and contrasting, and even evaluating the authenticity of a source. These strategies help learners make sense of the resources used to answer their questions and connect prior knowledge with new knowledge, often creating more questions as learners work toward the learning outcome.

Context for New Meaning

When learners make connections to prior learning, context is developed for constructing new meaning. For beginning researchers, this process might require more direct instruction or guidance to help learners see those connections. As learners become more comfortable with questioning as part of their learning, making these context connections will also become more innate. Once questioning becomes part of the culture of inquiry in the school, these connections will be easier and more relevant to the learners.

The following inquiry tools help school librarians and other educators collaborate to design inquiry opportunities that activate "learners' prior and background knowledge as context for constructing new meaning" (AASL 2018, School Librarian I.A.2.).

QFT

The Right Question Institute has an online planning tool to help educators develop a QFT for their inquiry units. Through a step-by-step process, school librarians can design an inquiry unit that uses questions as the basis for meeting the learning objectives of the inquiry unit. "The first half of the tool asks questions such as, 'What are your teaching objectives for the lesson?' and 'why are you using the QFT in this lesson?'" ("Create a Question Formulation Technique Lesson Plan" 2017). Working through the online tool helps refine collaborative lesson design that will engage curiosity and initiative as well as help learners create new meaning for content areas being studied. The online tool will guide educators through the QFT process, helping school librarians and educator partners create lesson plans that can be used immediately.

ESSENTIAL QUESTIONS

Essential Questions allow learners to engage with content-area subjects and pursue knowledge based on personal interests. Essential Questions allow learners opportunities to investigate, ask questions, and engage curiosity, leading to knowledge application. TeachThought has examples of Essential Questions to begin an inquiry unit. These examples of Essential Questions are broken down into large themes such as Decisions, Actions, and Consequences; Social Justice, Culture, Beliefs, and Rituals; Adversity, Conflict, and Change; Utopia and Dystopia; Chaos and Order; and many more. Once the overall theme of the learning unit is decided, using these examples can help frame the inquiry so that all learners can work through the unit with success. These questions provide a means to model questioning so that learners can make connections between new learning and prior knowledge.

NEED TO KNOW LIST

After facilitating learners' creation of a Need to Know List, revisiting the list often helps guide learners and reinforce inquiry skills throughout the overall unit of study. During the unit, the educator builds check-ins to evaluate whether the learners feel that they can answer the questions. The educator decides how to proceed—whether to review, coach in small groups, or incorporate support into the lessons that follow. Learners are empowered because they determine when a topic is fully addressed or needs more work (McCarthy 2016). If learners are struggling with making connections and gaining context for the learning unit, the school librarian and classroom educator can develop, reteach, and model lessons to help learners gain or use the right information through questioning and to make those connections, gaining context for new learning.

K-W-L CHART

The National Education Association (NEA) has good strategies to help frame learners' thinking when using the inquiry process and K-W-L charts. For *K,* NEA gives these educator prompts: "Have questions ready to help students brainstorm their ideas. Sometimes students need more prompting than, *'Tell me everything you know about _____,'* to get them started." Or "Encourage students to explain their associations. This is especially important for those associations that are vague or unusual. Ask, *'What made you think of that?'*" (NEA 2017; italics added). This modeling gives learners a chance to begin to make connections to their prior knowledge.

NEA continues with asking alternative questions for generating ideas for the *W* column in a K-W-L chart.

> If, in response to "What do you want to learn about this topic?" your [learners] are either having trouble coming up with ideas, or are saying, "nothing," try asking one of the following questions instead: *"What do you think you will learn about this topic from the text you will be reading?"* . . . [Or] come prepared with your own questions to add to the *W* column. You might want [learners] to focus on ideas in the text [that their own questions are not likely to lead them to]. Be sure not to add too many of your own questions, however. The majority of the questions in the *W* column should be student-generated." (NEA 2017)

Personalizing the questions in the *W* column engages learners to want to know more because the questions are based on their interests and curiosity.

For *L,* NEA suggests to "encourage students to write in the *L* column anything they found especially interesting. To distinguish between the answers to their questions and the ideas they found interesting, have [learners] code the information in their *L* columns. For example, they can put a check mark next to the information that answers questions from the *K* column. And they can put a star next to ideas that they found interesting" (NEA 2017). Using this structured protocol allows learners to engage their curiosity and make connections to prior knowledge as context for new learning.

SEE, THINK, WONDER

The See, Think, Wonder protocol introduces what an inquiry culture looks like and teaches learners to communicate and collaborate effectively in order to develop the critical-thinking skills necessary for longer inquiry units (Ritchhart, Church, and Morrison 2011, 55–58). See, Think, Wonder is especially effective when looking at primary sources or doing research about artists. With this protocol, using a primary source picture or painting from the Library of Congress is a great way to connect learners with different mediums or information formats, engaging learners who are visual and kinesthetic learners or learners who have language or learning barriers to textual information.

HOW MIGHT WE AND THE 5 WHYS METHOD

Because both the How Might We and the 5 Whys protocols work with Design Thinking, using them for specific STEAM or makerspace units challenges learners to go beyond what they already know about a particular subject. Throw out a design challenge to learners and have them decide on problem areas that need to be solved. Then reframe learners' questions as How Might We questions. The questions become opportunities for design. This process can be done using sticky notes or a technology tool such as Padlet to generate lots of ideas for solutions that can be grouped together to solve the design challenge. The 5 Whys method would be good for creating community change (class, school, local community, etc.).

Fostering Curiosity and Initiative

School librarians can foster curiosity and initiative by working with Appreciative Inquiry. Whitney and Trosten-Bloom offered tips for how to coach learners using Appreciative Inquiry in this manner.

First, create opportunities for equal voice and help learners speak from the "inside out." This approach creates the inquiry community atmosphere "where all voices have value, even the ones whose voices are often not heard," and builds on personal interest and curiosity (Whitney and Trosten-Bloom 2010, 107).

Second, keep the focus on the affirmative. Approaching challenges or problems through an affirmation model—"When we were researching last time, what sources did we find that worked well? Do you think we can use them again?"—builds the disposition to carry on as well as apply a transferable skill to other learning experiences.

Third, "give away the power." Help learners build metacognitive skills to grow in their learning and gain confidence that they as learners can succeed.

And last, make sure learners succeed. Did the educator team build in enough scaffolds so that learners can meet the learning target with support but mostly on their own?

Fostering curiosity and initiative in learners requires lots of advance planning on the part of the school librarian and the classroom or content educator. However, the benefits of learners' engaging in inquiry because of that planning will lead to better outcomes that truly demonstrate learning and reflect transferable knowledge skills.

"By designing opportunities to share the benefits and products of inquiry learning with all stakeholders, including school administrators and parents, the school librarian becomes a valuable instructional leader and partner focused on engagement and deep authentic learning" (AASL 2018, 71).

Questions for the Reflective Practitioner

1. How can I encourage other educators to collaborate with me and incorporate questioning into content-area subject units?

2. How can using the questioning tools and protocols outlined in this chapter help me collaborate with other educators so that learners have an opportunity to practice asking questions and making connections with prior knowledge as context for new meaning?

3. In what other ways do (or can) I work with other educators to model inquiry and aid learners' growth in the inquiry process?

6

Transforming School Libraries into Inquiry Labs

ow do educators engage learners with core content? How can learners then take that new knowledge and apply it to a real-world situation? What is the most important thing a learner needs to know in order to answer a question? These considerations come before all educators as they begin to plan any lesson or unit for learners. And *always* on the learner's mind is the "why" question: why are we doing this assignment, this test, this project? If school librarians and other educators can start by answering this why question, answers to the other questions will fall into place. But how does that learning happen? Collaborative learning opportunities developed in partnership by school librarians and other educators are the most effective way to create engaging and relevant inquiry units for learners to gain knowledge about curricular content and information literacy skills.

"The school library establishes an inquiry culture that permeates all facets of learners' lives by engaging learner curiosity and bolstering learners' initiative" (AASL 2018, 72). Whether maintaining an updated collection, collaborating with educator partners, or providing professional development for other educators about inquiry, the school librarian uses the school library space as the model for inquiry-based learning for both the personal and academic growth of all learners.

Enabling Curiosity

To effectively enable curiosity and initiative in learners and integrate learner Competencies into instruction, school librarians need to make sure that when they are collaborating with other educators, they are "embedding the inquiry process within grade bands and within disciplines" (AASL 2018, School Library, I.A.1.). School librarians can facilitate this action by using a number of different inquiry-based process models. The following examples demonstrate ways to integrate the School Library Alignments in the Inquire Think Domain when collaborating on a unit using an inquiry process model.

GID

In GID, the Open, Immerse, and Explore phases set the groundwork for curiosity and initiative. Once those stages have been planned and developed by the teaching team, learners will identify an area of focus that interests them and that will propel them through the remaining processes.

One example of this process, shared on the blog *52 Weeks of Guided Inquiry,* involved secondary learners in a poetry unit that featured a poet reciting his own work as the Open phase of the unit. This unit asked learners to expand their thinking about their experience of hearing poetry. Learners were asked to research slam poems, music lyrics, or other rhythmic poems that were shared in small-group Inquiry Circles. This phase led learners to identify and develop a research question about poetry. Learners were given voice and choice in how they displayed their new learning (Steere 2018). This secondary-level example enables engagement and curiosity within the English language arts curriculum by embedding an inquiry process model.

Another blog post discussed second graders studying famous Americans. The school librarian began her Open phase with tangible artifacts about each person being studied, and learners used prior knowledge to guess to whom the artifacts belonged. During the Immerse and Explore phases, the school librarian had learners use an inquiry log to research several people they were interested in knowing more about. From there learners narrowed down their findings to a final choice for further research, ultimately presenting the contributions of their famous American to their peers (Hutcherson 2017). Working collaboratively with a social studies educator, the school librarian was able to improve integration of a systematic search process in the curriculum.

BIG6

In stage 1 of the Big6 model, Task Definition, school librarians begin to enable curiosity and initiative within an inquiry lesson. Having learners identify what they need to know through observation and questioning begins the inquiry process.

For example, in the lesson "Plan, Do, Review . . . What Is Bugging You?," Pre-K–2 learners use the scientific method to learn about bugs through observation (fieldwork), class discussion, and debriefing (Benson, n.d.). Using fiction and nonfiction titles (e.g., *The Grouchy Ladybug* by Eric Carle and *Are You a Ladybug?* by Judy Allen), the educator begins the inquiry process with story. Learners develop questions based on what they learn from the stories, leading to fieldwork outside and an art lesson to demonstrate learning. This unit embeds the inquiry process model within disciplines by highlighting English language arts, science, and art curriculums to engage curiosity through questioning.

For older learners, Big6 features an extension lesson for studying the Civil War and Reconstruction (Berkowitz, n.d.). Learners review and extend their knowledge of the period by researching social, political, or economic perspectives of key historical figures to prepare and present knowledge in a roundtable discussion. This lesson engages learners' curiosity and initiative because this lesson is done after the initial content-area lesson by the content-area educator and provides learners opportunities to apply what they learned in an extension lesson in which critical thinking, collaboration, and communication can be assessed along with the application of new knowledge.

STRIPLING MODEL OF INQUIRY

To enable curiosity and initiative using the Stripling model, focus on the Connect and Wonder phases. As with the GID example, placing artifacts, photos, and primary source items on tables so learners can begin asking questions and making connections to prior knowledge is one way to pave the way into the Investigate and Construct phases. Learners will choose an artifact, photo, or primary source document that appeals to them and complete a protocol like See, Think, Wonder. As learners build on their Wonder questions, they can use a concept map to help plan out their question generation and narrow their questions to one central question that will drive the inquiry forward.

PATHWAYS TO KNOWLEDGE

The Pathways to Knowledge model enables curiosity and initiative through the Appreciation and Presearch stages. In their book, Pappas and Tepe provided the following two examples that showcase how school librarians and other educators can create inquiry units to support curiosity and initiative. For Appreciation, a seventh-grade educator showed learners Native American murals that depicted everyday life for those tribes. Learners were asked to pose questions about the different murals—style, materials used, choices about what was painted, and so on. This curiosity led their inquiry about this art form as well as what the art said about Native American life, integrating social studies and art curriculums.

For Presearch, elementary learners studied animal habitats—where animals live and why they choose those places. The learners had observed a pond, a forest, and a park that were near the school, but their classroom educator and the school librarian knew that the learners needed to go broader. Learners brainstormed more habitats and elements within those habitats, using an online encyclopedia along with K-W-L charts and webbing graphic organizer activities, thus integrating the inquiry process within curriculum disciplines (Pappas and Tepe 2002, 4–7).

Inquiry Integration

As school districts move away from using high-stakes testing as a means of evaluating learners, many districts are returning to using PBL as a way to blend traditional teaching tools with experiences that are more learner-centric. PBL prepares learners "for academic, personal, and career success, and readies young people to rise to the challenges of their lives and the world they will inherit. . . . Students develop deep content knowledge as well as critical thinking, creativity, and communication skills in the context of doing an authentic, meaningful project" (PBLWorks, n.d.). PBL begins with a Driving Question that asks learners to develop a Need to Know List, which drives how inquiry is used throughout the unit to engage learners. "The school library enables curiosity and initiative by using a systematic instructional-development and information-search process in working with other educators to improve integration of the process into curriculum" (AASL 2018, School Library I.A.2.).

NEED TO KNOW LIST

To begin the PBL process, a challenging problem or Driving Question is presented that engages and sustains learners through an inquiry process to solve the problem and apply new knowledge as part of their demonstration of learning.

A Driving Question for an elementary history, social science, and language arts project on U.S. regions might be this: "How do other regions in the United States influence my life?" To answer this question, learners might create a show segment for *The Amazing Race* for another class. A science question for secondary grades that will help learners better understand the observation process while using the scientific method might be this one: "How do observations lead us to conclusions?" (MyPBLWorks, n.d.). These types of Driving Questions are used to sustain curiosity and initiative. Driving Questions must be broad enough to allow for convergent and divergent thinking (they are not "Googleable"). The questions must also tie to the learning objectives and be engaging enough that learners can develop suitable questions to answer the Driving Question and present their learning.

QFT

Just as the Driving Question for PBL leads to a Need to Know List, the QFT supports learners in developing their own questions to stimulate new learning. Following are two examples of the QFT in action from the Right Question Institute.

Jennifer Shaffer from Frederick County Public Schools in Walkersville, Maryland, "showed her students the QFocus—a picture of an alligator with baby alligators on its head. The room 'erupted' with their questions and she recorded their questions and allowed them to whisper their final question to their partner. The class then used their questions as they were reading a nonfiction text about alligators" (RQI 2018).

An example for the secondary level from Laura Mercier at McComb School District in McComb, Mississippi, used a quote from the nonfiction text *Warriors Don't Cry* as the QFocus: "By volunteering, Melba took the first step to desegregate an all-white school." Learners walked through the QFT to record what they already knew about segregation and to identify what they needed to know about how to bring about social change. By engaging learners' curiosity about segregation, McComb was able to show learners how to engage with text (RQI 2018).

ESSENTIAL QUESTIONS

Essential Questions support ongoing, engaging inquiry that leads to transferable skills and to more learning. The Global Digital Citizen Foundation has created a list of more than one hundred Essential Questions that meet the definition and format described by Wiggins and McTighe. Following are some examples of good Essential Questions from that list (Watanabe-Crockett 2017):

Math/Computer Science
- How can I best represent a pattern using mathematical principles? (Elementary)
- What ways can mathematical problems conceal as much as they reveal? (Secondary)

Arts
- How does a song, piece of art, or a dance communicate with us? (Elementary)
- What do we mean when we refer to music as the *universal language*? (Secondary)

Health/Wellness
- Why (and how) does choosing activities we enjoy contribute to our whole-being health? (Elementary)
- What is special about how you deal with personal conflicts and change, and how could this help someone else? (Secondary)

SEE, THINK, WONDER

The See, Think, Wonder protocol is wonderful for media literacy lessons, especially in helping learners determine bias. This critical-thinking skill is important in today's world for discerning fake news and propaganda in media. The organization Facing History and Ourselves has wonderful media literacy lessons to help learners discern bias in media.

The lesson entitled "Analyzing Nazi Propaganda" uses Essential Questions tied to critical thinking (How can propaganda influence individuals' attitudes and actions?) as well as history and social science content (How did the Nazis create "in" groups and "out" groups in German society?). This lesson asks learners to "follow a procedure to analyze an image by first observing details and gathering other helpful information about the image before interpreting its meaning . . . [and] understand that media messages are often carefully crafted to elicit specific feelings and attitudes from an audience and to persuade people to take particular actions" (Facing History and Ourselves 2018). Using a primary source image, learners engage in the See, Think, Wonder protocol to develop questions that will lead them to understand how images can influence society for better or worse.

WHY? WHAT IF? HOW? AND HOW MIGHT WE

The How? Why? What If? and the How Might We protocols are great to use for STEAM challenges and projects as well as for design challenges in your makerspaces. Begin with questions as simple as "Why does a kite need wind in order to fly?" or "What if we could build a better bridge?" or "How might we build a better robot?" Using Appreciative Inquiry here opens learners' minds to possibility when questions are geared toward making something better or finding out why something worked versus why it didn't. Keeping these challenges open-ended allows learners to hone in on an aspect of the problem or challenge that interests them.

5 WHYS METHOD

The 5 Whys method is great for working with other educators who want to make a change in instruction, policy, culture, or the like. School librarians can use this method when working with learners in an advisory role related to making programming and services in the school library better for everyone. This protocol is also great to use when working to establish what is needed to create the culture of inquiry.

Extending the Inquiry Process

Inquiry processes are not limited to what can be done in the school library. The role that school librarians can play in integrating the Inquire Think Domain throughout grade levels and content disciplines is to model lessons in the school library and to conduct professional development for and with their educator partners. Other inquiry methods can extend the inquiry process beyond work that can be done in the school library. For example, Socratic seminars, fishbowl discussions, roundtables, debates, and other presentation forms are all ways to transfer learning and to apply the learning in new situations for summative assessment of knowledge, skills, and understandings for content.

Professional development for educators about the inquiry process should be a part of the school library. These professional development or information sessions can be presented one-on-one, in small groups, in large groups, or even through modules for a blended learning, on-demand experience.

Because the school library is used by all learners and educators in a school community, it is imperative that the school library and school librarian take an active role in developing and sustaining an inquiry culture that enables curiosity and initiative through supports and integration in the curriculum across grade bands and within disciplines.

Questions for the Reflective Practitioner

1. How can I provide professional development to other educators in a way that helps integrate the inquiry process into grade levels and content areas?

2. In what ways can I encourage my most resistant educator colleagues to try collaborating with me to connect core content to inquiry-based curriculum?

3. What successful examples of collaborative planning and integration of inquiry processes do I already have with content areas or grade bands, and how do I leverage those to expand my circle of collaborators?

THINK in Practice

ow do school librarians assist other educators and learners with discovery? Co-planning and implementing units that engage learners from the beginning motivate learners to want to know more about the content that learners need to learn. The strategies, tools, and example lessons included here inspire learners to become curious and use initiative to work through inquiry units from start to finish. These examples demonstrate how and when the Think Domain is being used in the research process to build Competencies in the Shared Foundation of Inquire.

No-Tech Tools

When time is limited or when working with younger learners, no-tech solutions to aid question generation may be beneficial. For younger learners whose literacy skills aren't as well developed, having the educator or school librarian become the scribe using chart paper, whiteboard, and markers to capture learner-developed questions with an inquiry process model can provide visible thinking for learners at the beginning of the inquiry process and help them focus on the content and questions while staying engaged. For older learners, a no-tech option may begin with learners individually or in small groups jotting down questions on notebook paper and then categorizing and prioritizing the questions as a larger group. Several no-tech thinking routines from Project Zero's Visible Thinking Network can be used to support learners in formulating questions (Harvard Project Zero, n.d.b).

ZOOM IN

Use the Zoom In thinking routine when the goals for learners are to narrow their focus, zoom in on specific elements, and make inferences. Present learners with a small section of an image and ask, "What do you see or notice?" and "What is your hypothesis or interpretation of what this might be?" Then as more of the image is revealed, ask learners to continue their brainstorming by answering these questions: "What new things do you see?" "How does this change your hypothesis or interpretation?" "Has the information answered any of your wonders or changed your previous ideas?" "What new thing are you wondering?"

Repeat the reveal-and-question process until the whole image is revealed and learners have answered this final question: "What lingering questions remain for you about this image?" (Ritchhart et al., 2011, 64). Through this routine, learners come to the realizations that thinking is a process and that as new information and understandings are revealed, minds can be changed.

THINK/PUZZLE/EXPLORE

The Think/Puzzle/Explore routine is helpful when beginning a topic and when you want learners to develop their own questions of investigation. Have learners brainstorm ideas about the inquiry topic by answering these three questions: "What do you *think* you know about this topic?" "What questions or *puzzles* do you have?" "How can you *explore* this topic?" (Ritchhart et al., 2011, 71).

CHALK TALK

The Chalk Talk routine helps build a collaborative thinking routine for learners. Using chart paper, the school librarian asks learners to write or draw their answers to these questions: "What ideas come to mind when you consider this idea, question, or problem?" "What connections can you make to others' responses?" "What questions arise as you think about the ideas and consider the responses and comments of others?" (Ritchhart et al., 2011, 78). Creating visual thinking for an idea or process helps learners identify and make connections to the topic being studied.

3-2-1 BRIDGE

The 3-2-1 Bridge routine asks learners to uncover their initial thoughts, ideas, questions, and understandings about a topic and then to connect these to new thinking about the topic after they have received some instruction. Whenever new information is gained, bridges can be built between new ideas and prior understandings. The focus is on understanding and connecting one's thinking, rather than pushing it toward a specific outcome (Ritchhart et al., 2011, 86).

RED LIGHT, YELLOW LIGHT

The Red Light, Yellow Light routine is good to employ when learners enter the early research stages (Explore, Location and Access, Wonder, and Presearch noted in several of the inquiry process models discussed in earlier chapters). As learners read, view, or listen to resources, they should keep in mind the following questions and record their reflections in a paper graphic organizer: "What are the red lights here? That is, what things stop you in your tracks as a learner because you doubt its accuracy?" "What are your yellow lights here? That is, what things slow you down a bit, give you pause and make you wonder if they are true and accurate or not?" (Ritchhart et al., 2011, 185).

CLAIM-SUPPORT-QUESTION

The Claim-Support-Question routine is best used when learners are ready to begin synthesizing information. Inquiry logs, sticky notes, graphic organizers, and other paper tools can be used to help facilitate this routine. Ask learners to make a claim about their topic or explain what is being examined about the issue or idea being researched. Learners should then provide support for their claim using evidence found during the inquiry process. Review their support information and ask learners several follow-up questions such as, "What may make you doubt the claim? What seems left hanging? What isn't fully explained? What further ideas or issues does your claim raise?" The answers to these questions provide learners a map for going back to fill in their knowledge gaps (Ritchhart et al., 2011, 191).

Low-Tech Tools

Low-tech tools allow learners to receive instant feedback from school librarians and educators. If you choose to include low-tech tools in your programming, be sure to choose technology tools that aid or further learning and not just use technology for technology's sake. Low-tech tools are easy to insert into many word-processing programs within Microsoft, Google, or Apple or as discussion questions on a learning management platform. Some low-tech tools that enable curiosity and initiative in learners include online questioning graphic organizers; back channels; online discussion boards; surveys, polling, and data collection; and interactive feedback. Diana Neebe and Jen Roberts, authors of *Power Up: Making the Shift to 1:1 Teaching and Learning* (2015), have favorite sites for each of these categories.

ONLINE QUESTIONING GRAPHIC ORGANIZERS

ReadWriteThink has lots of online graphic organizers that learners can work through and then either print or e-mail to their classroom educator or school librarian. These low-tech tools assist learners in connecting prior and background knowledge and can be used quickly during short inquiry units.

BACK CHANNELS

Back channels provide a digital location for learners to talk about their learning and for educators to make real-time assessments as learners question and comment back and forth to each other. Google Docs, Nearpod, Padlet, and Backchannel Chat are free online tools by which learners can engage with each other through an inquiry process. Educators can create an account and share the link with learners without worry about violating the Children's Online Privacy Protection Act (COPPA) or the Family Educational Rights and Privacy Act (FERPA).

ONLINE DISCUSSION BOARDS

Online discussion boards extend the inquiry process beyond the time learners are in school and expand learning to allow for "Ahas" or questions that come up when learners revisit their work at home. Collaborize Classroom and Schoology are two platforms free to educators on which they can create accounts that only their learners can access for online discussion. Online discussion boards allow learners to make connections to their own and others' prior background knowledge as they move through the inquiry process.

SURVEYS, POLLING, AND DATA COLLECTION

Google Forms, SurveyMonkey, and Poll Everywhere are free services for creating surveys and polls to engage learners and model inquiry processes. If your school district has a learning management system, it may include a polling option as well.

 ## High-Tech Tools

If your school district has a well-developed blended learning platform and learners are able to access tools that allow them to showcase new learning to a more-global audience, these tools can help learners do just that. The high-tech tools described here are from AASL's Best Websites for Teaching and Learning and help learners demonstrate the Think Domain, but they could be added to any educator's toolbox. Use what is approved by your school or district.

CLASSHOOK

ClassHook, a video-based website, helps you find clips from popular television shows and movies. Use this site as part of the QFT and the See, Think, Wonder protocols to enable curiosity and initiative. ClassHook can be used to engage learners to activate their "prior and background knowledge as context for constructing new meaning" (AASL 2018, School Librarian I.A.2.) by using popular culture as a beginning connection to prior learning and new content about to be studied.

GOOGLE KEEP

Google Keep is an online tool to use with bookmarking, note taking, and setting reminders. Google Keep creates a visible Thinking Map as learners move through an inquiry process and can provide real-time assessment opportunities for classroom educators and school librarians.

FLIPGRID

Flipgrid is a tool for gathering conversation topics and discussion whereby learners respond to an inquiry prompt via video in ninety seconds, from anywhere, using just about any device. Microsoft has made this tool free for educators. Flipgrid will aid learners in making connections to learning by using oral communication skills to speak about a personal or academic topic.

BEYONDPAD

Use Beyondpad for an easy and efficient way to organize, structure, and keep track of notes. Part whiteboard, part digital sticky notes, this organization and management style site gives learners and their educators another way to present notes, ideas, and information. Like Google Keep, Beyondpad allows the school librarian and classroom educator to have real-time information about the thinking processes of learners as they move through the inquiry unit.

AYOA

Ayoa (formerly called DropTask) is a task management tool that provides a colorful visual of the user's task at hand resembling a Venn diagram. The free version allows collaboration between two people on five projects. Collaborators can upload files, assign tasks, track progress, and communicate with one another. After creating the needed steps and due dates of the project, each collaborator marks completed tasks, and task progress can be tracked through the activity view and notification system.

Example Lesson Plans for Think

The following lesson plans promote content-area collaboration and are aligned to Think Domain Competencies. These lessons feature the options of no-tech, low-tech, and high-tech tools and can be adapted to meet the needs of your learners, educator partners, and school library environment.

INQUIRY AND THE SQUID

Grade Levels: K–2

Contributor: Jennifer Cooper

This lesson engages learners' curiosity and initiative using science concepts for inquiry and questioning. Using a funny picture book about the giant squid, learners will think like a scientist by asking questions about a large sea animal. As learners work to answer their questions, they begin to understand ethical use of information by "thanking the author" (citing the source) who provided the information.

"I Can" Statement

I can find information about a topic using appropriate and available resources.

AASL Standards Framework for Learners

I.A.1. Learners display curiosity and initiative by formulating questions about a personal interest or a curricular topic.

I.A.2. Learners display curiosity and initiative by recalling prior and background knowledge as context for new meaning.

Content Areas

Language Arts
Science/STEM/STEAM

Duration

Two 45-minute class sessions

Materials

- *I'm the Biggest Thing in the Ocean* by Kevin Sherry
- Inquiry process poster (GID, Big6, Stripling, Pathways to Knowledge)
- Graphic organizer
- Printed encyclopedia entries or articles about giant squid

Lesson Day 1

Before: Ask learners about the animal on the cover of the book, *I'm the Biggest Thing in the Ocean.* Explain that the animal is a giant squid and that the class will use the inquiry process to learn about the squid.

During: Using an inquiry process poster, share with learners the different steps involved in the inquiry process but focus on Questioning. Ask learners to brainstorm what they would like to know about the giant squid. Record their answers. Read the book aloud to the class.

Assessment: Ask learners if they have any additional questions about the giant squid after reading the book.

Lesson Day 2

Before: Ask learners about the book read during the previous class session and what they remember about the giant squid.

During: Read the questions created during the previous class period together as a group. Tell learners, "The next step is to collect information to answer our questions and then say thank you to our information source." Pass out the graphic organizer and printed encyclopedia entries or articles about the giant squid. Work through the first three questions together. Make sure to complete the crediting step—thanking the encyclopedia for the answers. Ask learners to individually or in pairs use the article to complete the graphic organizer, answering the last two questions.

Assessment: Review the last two completed questions to determine learners' comprehension of the information. Ask learners to verbally repeat the steps taken to find information—what steps they took to initiate the search, which source they used, how they found the answer using text features. If the school library has interactive technology such as a SMART Board, a Promethean Board, or touchscreen monitors, assess fine motor skills and whether learners can use the technology in tandem with the search strategies. If learners worked in groups or pairs to develop their questions, assess how well learners communicated and collaborated in the creation of questions. Learners should be able to state why questions are important to their learning and why questions they ask are important.

SHOULD A TIGER BE A PET?

Grade Levels: 3–5

Contributors: Heather Hess, Caroline Romano, Rita Saylor, Sue Strada, and Donald Walutes

This lesson is the beginning of a larger inquiry unit about animals and how they impact learners' lives and the world. Focusing on the best pets for people, this inquiry uses an online encyclopedia or website article. Learners will focus on getting facts to answer a research question and will learn how to use a citation tool to annotate and cite a source. Using information found in the article, learners will apply their new knowledge to discuss what it takes to be a responsible pet owner and what the right kinds of pets are for their families.

"I Can" Statements

I can annotate and cite an article in NoodleTools.
I can participate in a Socratic seminar about pets.

AASL Standards Framework for Learners

I.A.1. Learners display curiosity and initiative by formulating questions about a personal interest or a curricular topic.

I.A.2. Learners display curiosity and initiative by recalling prior and background knowledge as context for new meaning.

Content Areas
Language Arts
Science/STEM/STEAM

Duration
Four 45-minute class sessions

Materials
- "Should a Tiger Be Your Pet?" EBSCO article (or any story or article about getting a pet)
- NoodleTools or another online citation tool

Lesson

Before: Ask learners, "Why is it important to have facts when we want to persuade someone? How do we get facts? What do we do to show where our facts came from?"

During: Share the question, "Should a tiger be your pet?" Using the article from the online database, talk about using nonfiction articles to get facts. Model how to cite the article in NoodleTools. Then ask learners to read and annotate the article in NoodleTools listing facts about whether or not a tiger would make a good pet. Using the facts found in the article, lead learners in a discussion about tigers as pets. Encourage learners to use inferencing skills to talk about caring for pets and which pet would be the best type for them. Facilitate a Socratic seminar using these questions: "What kind of relationship should people have with a pet?" "What responsibility do you have for taking care of pets for life?"

Assessment: Assess learners on their ability to navigate a citation tool, to create the citation, and to write an annotation about the book. Alternatively, assess work to prepare for the Socratic seminar, such as outlining, storyboarding, question drafting, and so on. Assess how learners use their communication and critical-thinking skills during the seminar. Further assessment areas could include active listening skills and how well learners respond to each other.

MONEY AND CREDIT

Grade Levels: 3–5

Contributor: Lori Donovan

This lesson introduces economic terms to learners by using a picture book. Understanding other ways of obtaining goods and services beyond money is sometimes difficult for learners. The many types of goods and services are also complex for younger learners. This lesson will introduce and reinforce economic terms for elementary learners.

"I Can" Statement

I can interpret graphs, charts, and pictures to determine how goods, services, and money are used.

AASL Standards Framework for Learners

I.A.1. Learners display curiosity and initiative by formulating questions about a personal interest or a curricular topic.

I.A.2. Learners display curiosity and initiative by recalling prior and background knowledge as context for new meaning.

Content Areas

History/Social Science

Duration

One 45-minute class session

Materials

- *A New Coat for Anna* by Harriet Ziefert
- An online database of economic terms
- Graphic organizer using economic terms (e.g., *trade, barter, natural resource, capital resource, human resource*)
- History of Money from www.banksite.com/kidscorner/history.htm

Lesson

Before: Ask learners, "What are goods and services? How do we get those goods and services? What happens if we don't have money to buy goods and services?"

During: Read *A New Coat for Anna,* stopping during the reading to talk about why Anna couldn't get a new coat and to lead a discussion about bartering and trade. After reading the story, review natural, capital, and human resources using the History of Money site and list examples of these resources on chart paper or with a projection system. Ask learners to complete the graphic organizer using examples from the story and an online database of economic terms.

Assessment: Assess learners on how well they navigated the databases to answer the graphic organizer.

ECONOMICS THROUGH PICTURE BOOKS

Grade Levels: 6–8

Contributor: Debi Graves

This economics lesson asks learners to expand their knowledge with more-advanced concepts, including buying and selling as part of entrepreneurship and the role the Federal Reserve plays in national economics. Learners will work through a series of stations using print and digital materials to access and use information. At the end of the module, learners will practice citing sources to document where they found answers to their questions.

"I Can" Statement
I can identify basic economic systems.

AASL Standards Framework for Learners
I.A.2. Learners display curiosity and initiative by recalling prior and background knowledge as context for new meaning.

Content Areas
Language Arts
History/Social Science
Science/STEM/STEAM

Duration
One 90-minute class session

Materials
- Nonfiction picture books about the following economics topics: taxes, supply and demand, entrepreneurship, saving and borrowing, goods and services, competition, and the Federal Reserve
- Online databases, Discovery Education, or other streaming service
- Learning management software such as Blackboard, Canvas, Schoology, NearPod, or other module software
- Chromebooks

Lesson
Before: Prepare learners with vocabulary and basic economic structures. Pull print and online resources covering each of the topics. Set up a station for each topic and distribute resources accordingly.

During: Allow time for learners to navigate through stations answering specific economics questions in modules in the learning management software. Ask learners to complete question sheets using print sources and online databases about economics terms.

Assessment: Assess learners on how well they navigated the databases to answer questions. Other assessment ideas for this small unit include how well learners used the academic vocabulary to answer questions and explain concepts. To extend the lesson, have learners create their own economics stories to share at the elementary level. This strategy would be a good summative assessment for the educator partner to determine how well learners took in the new information.

THE IMPACT OF THE CIVIL WAR

Grade Levels: 6–8

*Contributors: Diana Garbera, Leslie Vaughn,
and Pam Rockenbach*

This lesson uses a learning management system such as Blackboard, Canvas, or Schoology. Learners work on this assignment in the school library and at home using the library databases. Working with historical and primary sources about Reconstruction, learners find answers to questions and make inferences about the effects (social and economic) of the aftermath of the Civil War on different types of people at the time of Reconstruction. Learners work through modules that include graphic organizers, questioning protocols, and inference sheets. As learners follow the inquiry process, the school librarian and content educator will see who needs more support and which learners progress quickly, giving them an opportunity to complete extended challenges.

"I Can" Statement

I can demonstrate knowledge of the effects of Reconstruction on American life.

AASL Standards Framework for Learners

I.A.2. Learners display curiosity and initiative by recalling prior and background knowledge as context for new meaning.

Content Areas

History/Social Science

Duration

One 90-minute class session

Materials

- Nonfiction and reference texts about Reconstruction
- Online databases, Discovery Education, or other streaming service
- Learning management software such as Blackboard, Canvas, Schoology, NearPod, or other module software
- Chromebooks

Lesson

Before: In collaboration with the classroom educator, create a module that includes print, digital, and primary sources about Reconstruction. Make these materials available to learners in the school library. Before learners visit the school library, the classroom educator will present instruction about the Civil War and Reconstruction.

During: Explain to learners the different types of resources that they may use to complete the module and review how to cite sources. Learners will complete the module using print sources and online databases.

Assessment: Assess learners on how well they navigated the databases to answer questions and how well they used nonfiction text features (such as the table of contents, the index, bold words, captions, etc.) to answer questions. To extend the lesson, ask learners to craft questions about their resources and then have different groups or learners in other class periods quiz the learners on what they have learned. This strategy would be a good formative assessment for the educator partner to determine how well learners took in the new information.

GOOGLE LIKE A ROCK STAR

Grade Levels: 9–12

Contributor: Robbie Barber

This mini-lesson is designed to remind learners about effective searching tools when using Google. The school librarian will walk learners through tricks and strategies (Boolean logic, truncation, site search, etc.) to answer a research question effectively using Google.

"I Can" Statements

I can form a more succinct, more successful Google search.

In learning to use Google better, I can learn how to use similar research databases better.

AASL Standards Framework for Learners

I.A.1. Learners display curiosity and initiative by formulating questions about a personal interest or a curricular topic.

Content Areas

Language Arts
History/Social Science
Science/STEM/STEAM

Duration

One 90-minute class session

Materials

- Learner handout with Google search strategies (Default search settings, optional search settings, Boolean logic)
- Chrome browser on a device

Lesson

Before: Explain how Google's search algorithm works. For example, ask, "Did you know that when you type a complete sentence, Google ignores certain words?" Demonstrate a search and talk about the keywords Google chooses or guesses as users type.

During: Discuss Boolean logic: AND, OR, NOT. Use examples like "chocolate AND/ OR/NOT lollipop." Using AND means Tootsie Pops will appear in the results; OR produces any chocolate AND any lollipops; NOT will result in no chocolate, but root beer lollipops will be there. Show how Google handles Boolean logic. Ask learners to search for *Spider-Man 3* and to identify the tricks that could be used to make Google recognize the *3*. Ask the group to discuss their Google search for *Spider-Man 3*. What methods were successful?

Assessment: Assess learners on how well they navigated a Google search and how well they applied the criteria for authentic, accurate, and current information to the site chosen to answer the research question. Alternatively, assess learners on how well they used Boolean operators and completed a successful Google search as well as whether they identified an appropriate site to answer the research question.

SERIAL AND BANNED BOOKS— PODCASTING INQUIRY

Grade Levels: 9–12

Contributor: Brooksie Kramer

Learners practice rhetorical analysis by listening to season one of the podcast *Serial* while reading a book of their choice from the American Library Association's list of commonly banned and challenged books. The *Serial* podcast serves as a model for learners' final product, which is a podcast episode that builds a case for or against the banning of their chosen book. The lesson plan was crafted for Advanced Placement learners, though this project could be modified for regular-level learners.

"I Can" Statement

I can locate, synthesize, and ethically use valid sources to craft an argument in a podcast format for an authentic audience of my peers.

AASL Standards Framework for Learners

I.A.1. Learners display curiosity and initiative by formulating questions about a personal interest or a curricular topic.

I.A.2. Learners display curiosity and initiative by recalling prior and background knowledge as context for new meaning.

Content Areas

Language Arts
Project-Based Learning

Duration

6 weeks, with 2 weeks of direct inquiry practice and instruction dispersed throughout

Materials

- Access to *Serial* podcast (available through website, YouTube, podcasting apps)
- Banned book assignment sheet (created with educator partner)
- Citation guides for learners (print and digital options)
- Podcasting or audio recording software
- Online catalog, library databases
- Google Keep or other note-taking application

Lesson

Before: Introduce the project and show learners how to access the *Serial* podcast. Provide learners with a listening schedule: sixteen days provided for twelve episodes at approximately fifty minutes per episode. Lead a discussion of *Serial*—facts, rhetorical strategies, questions, and the like. Ask learners to take notes on the case details and evidence of rhetoric as they listen to the podcast series. During this time, learners will also select and read a banned or challenged book from the assignment sheet. As learners listen to the podcast and review rhetorical devices in their English classroom, they also enter into the inquiry process to discover more about the background of their book and the history of book banning in general.

During: Review searching strategies with learners and ask them to start gathering reliable sources about banned books and the titles they selected using the online catalog, Google Scholar, Advanced Search in Google, library databases, and the 800s section of the school library. Introduce the concept of an annotated bibliography and provide instruction on MLA style and how to effectively use an online citation maker or the Purdue Online Writing Lab (OWL) website. Learners will be using their inquiry sources as "interviews" as they create a podcast in the style of *Serial,* building their cases for why their chosen books should or should not be banned. After learners have had time to curate their sources and create Works Cited entries, review the assignment sheet and discuss the requirements for creating an effective podcast. Introduce the recording application that learners will use for recording their podcasts. Provide learners at least three class periods for working in the school library, with additional time after school and during flex periods built into the school day. Learners will submit links to their finished podcast recordings in a collaborative Google Doc.

Assessment: Assess learners throughout the unit. Evaluate learners as they work through the I-Search process using rubrics (there are many free online). Assess learners on how they evaluate and cite sources on banned books to create their podcasts. Rubrics for assessing the finished podcasts can be located online. Provide content rubrics to learners as well, allowing them to peer review podcasts from three classmates.

PART III

Create

7

Creating
Curious Learners

he best part of being a school librarian is the learner who asks, "Do you have . . . ?" It is always exciting to see that learners are excited about wanting to know more and that they know somewhere in the school library is the answer they are looking for! Engaging natural curiosity through the inquiry process helps learners then create products that show their learning. Learners benefit when they work within a learning community, "engaging in a structured inquiry-based research process in which they may struggle through questioning, reformulating, failing, rethinking problems, and deciding between solutions" (AASL 2018, 70). Applying critical and creative thinking as learners engage with new knowledge is a learning skill that can be fostered within the school library.

Natural curiosity or personal interest in a topic or subject is what drives learners to want to know more. The best way to engage curiosity is through questioning. Teaching learners how to ask questions with a purpose, and that different types of questions will reveal or provide different kinds of answers, should be done often and under the guidance of school librarians. This chapter will explore strategies for integrating the Inquire Create Domain within a learning unit to help learners engage with their new knowledge and identify which types of evidence will answer their questions. Following an inquiry process leads learners to use evidence to identify gaps in their learning and formulate a plan with scaffolds to close those gaps in order to create products worth sharing.

Using Evidence with Questioning

When asking learners to "[follow] a process that includes using evidence to investigate questions" (AASL 2018, Learner I.B.1.), it is important to set the stage for learners by providing opportunities to see and practice good questioning. School librarians need to show learners the value of questions—not just the questions asked by classroom educators and textbook materials but also the questions asked by the learners themselves. School librarians can model and foster curiosity through questioning. Using lower level, "thin" questions, such as, "Who invented the A-bomb?" along with higher level, "thick" questions, such as, "Has the proliferation of nuclear arsenals really ended the threat of nuclear war?" enables learners to see the value of all types of questions and in what situations these questions need to be used. Also, learners learn that the types of questions asked lead the direction of their research in content and in context. The following examples describe how inquiry research process models prompt learners to engage with knowledge and to use evidence when investigating questions.

GID

By modeling three types of questions in GID—information, choice, and probing—school librarians prepare learners to know what type of question is needed depending on the information that is needed. *Information questions* provide a sense of what the learner already knows. The learner then can build upon that knowledge to create context for new learning by using evidence from answered questions. *Choice questions* guide the direction of the conversation on a difficult topic. *Probing questions* open dialogue for opinions, feelings, and thoughts (Kuhlthau et al., 2015, 29).

Learners take time to investigate questions in the Open, Immerse, Explore, and Identify phases of the GID process. By developing and working through questions in the beginning phases of the process, learners understand that different types of information are needed at various stages in the learning unit, that questions will change and evolve as answers are found, and that more questions are created from their investigations.

BIG6

In the Big6 model, educators model for learners three levels of questioning: literal, interpretive, and applied questions. *Literal questions* ask learners to recall verbatim or in their own words material previously read or taught by the educator. *Interpretive questions* ask learners to mentally manipulate information previously learned to create an answer or to support an answer. *Applied questions* ask learners to apply their found information in new or unique ways (Eisenberg and Berkowitz 2014). The nature of the assignment, or where in the assignment learners are, will determine which of these questions are developed and answered by the learners.

During Task Definition, the first stage of the Big6 model, learners determine that a problem requires more information to be solved. Learners can then identify what kind of information is needed to solve the problem by developing a series of literal questions. Developing these questions helps learners see connections between their prior knowledge and new knowledge and helps learners formulate opinions or interpretive questions about the evidence they find. Learners look for patterns and comparisons within multiple resources that require thoughtful answers, not Googleable ones. The important part of this process is that the questions developed by learners need to be scaffolded by the school librarian to help learners meet the learning target. School librarians can scaffold question generation by using questioning tools such as the QFT, Why? What If? How?, and See, Think, Wonder. As learners locate resources that could answer their questions or provide evidence, school librarians aid learners through scaffolded lessons to help learners find the *right* resource.

STRIPLING MODEL OF INQUIRY

With the Stripling model, learner questions are developed in the early stages of the inquiry process. In the Connect stage of the Stripling model, learners begin to make connections between what they already know and what they need to know more about. Educator partners can begin this connection process during classroom time using anticipation guides, graphic organizers, K-W-L charts, and other means to engage learners with prior knowledge before coming into the school library to begin formal research. Making connections between prior knowledge and knowledge gaps leads learners into the Wonder stage in which hypotheses are formed based on question development. Using questioning tools, learners can practice question writing that pushes beyond comprehension and work their way up Bloom's taxonomy for questioning to application and interpretation, leading to new knowledge generation (Stripling 2003, 12).

Modeling questioning for learners as they enter the Wonder stage sets learners up for developing metacognitive skills that will carry learners through the learning unit. Developing questions before reading or researching helps the school librarian and the learners to know what learners know and do not know about the subject. To gather evidence from a variety of sources, learners use a Driving Question to develop a Need to Know List. Together, the class can brainstorm questions that each learner can then pursue for further research to make new meaning.

Asking questions such as "Why is this information important?" and "How does this information fit with what I already know?" models self-questioning, pushing learners beyond the literal into higher order thinking and questions. When looking for gaps in information, learners need to ask, "What information has been left out of this passage? Why? What is the author's purpose?" Questions like these prompt learners to begin to ask more questions that deal with information gaps from one resource to the next (Stripling 2003, 12).

PATHWAYS TO KNOWLEDGE

The Presearch stage in the Pathways to Knowledge model enables learners to develop questions so that they can begin to see relationships between their topic and their learning. At the end of the Presearch stage, learners need to develop an Essential Question that will guide them through the rest of the pathways. Using inquiry logs or mind maps helps learners to start with their questions, find answers, and develop more questions as connections are made, as learners find evidence through their investigations, and as they move forward to the next stage.

Scaffolding to Fill Knowledge Gaps

Learners realize as they work through an inquiry process model that research is not linear and not easy. That is why the prefix *re-* is added to the root word *search.* There are multiple steps in the research process that may get repeated as learners realize gaps in their learning, especially if new information contradicts what they already thought to be true or knew about the subject being researched. As part of creating new knowledge, "learners [must] value and foster ideas, and devise and implement plans to address gaps in knowledge" (AASL 2018, 70). Providing scaffolds in the inquiry research process supports learners in their journey as they continue onward to "[devise] and [implement] a plan to fill knowledge gaps" (AASL 2018, Learner I.B.2.). Scaffolds provide support to aid learners in building a disposition to persevere and maintain focus and curiosity throughout the learning unit.

GID

In GID, interventions are designed to help learners through the inquiry process in the Identify, Gather, and Create stages. As learners begin to move on from identifying their topic and developing initial questions for investigation, new questions should be emerging that connect learners' prior knowledge to new knowledge. Using four basic inquiry abilities, learners can then be scaffolded through the inquiry process as early as kindergarten, leading to middle and high school projects that are more independent and in which inquiry is more refined.

1. Recall: Learners reflect on the information that stands out in what they read or heard.
2. Summarize: Learners place information gathered in some order of relevance.
3. Paraphrase: Learners restate information gathered in some order of relevance.
4. Extend: Learners apply new knowledge in new and creative ways (Kuhlthau, Maniotes, and Caspari 2012, 136).

BIG6

In the Big6 model, the purpose of questioning becomes a guide for learners to move through the inquiry process. Questions engage and propel learners through application of content knowledge to make real-world connections (Eisenberg and Berkowitz, 2014). Once the problem and information needed have been defined (stage 1), learners use questions for Information Seeking (stage 2); they Locate and Access the information (stage 3) and then Use Information (stage 4). By modeling active learning and engaging with learners, the school librarian can help scaffold learners through these stages of inquiry. Asking themselves reflective questions, not only about the inquiry question but also about the process, will help learners identify and fill gaps in their learning before moving on to create products that demonstrate their learning: "Can I answer my own research question so that someone who isn't familiar with the topic would understand?" "Do I have a good plan to organize my information?" "Will my project include all the appropriate information available? If not, where else can I look?"

STRIPLING MODEL OF INQUIRY

As learners move through Wonder and Investigate to the Connect phase of the Stripling model, they work to find the best resources to gather information (Stripling 2003, 17). Learners can use strategies to question an author's purpose and credibility, especially if the information contradicts learners' prior knowledge. An inquiry log can be used as a think-aloud strategy to help make connections between multiple resources and prior knowledge. School librarians can help scaffold learning by using graphic organizers that work through text structures to help learners summarize and paraphrase their learning. When entering the Connect phase, educator-to-learner and learner-to-learner conferencing can aid in finding gaps in knowledge and beginning to compare evidence to hypotheses to generate new explanations using the See, Think, Wonder protocol.

PATHWAYS TO KNOWLEDGE

Learners now move into the Search and Interpretation stages of the Pathways to Knowledge inquiry process model. Learners will identify resources that help answer the research question developed in the Presearch stage. Learners develop a plan, perhaps using a graphic organizer to list possible sources and then marking those sources as a yes or no after evaluating them. As learners move into the Interpretation stage, they begin to analyze, synthesize, and evaluate the information found to create new knowledge. Learners also reflect on where they are in the process to determine if they need to search more or if they are ready to move into the Communication stage. Graphic organizers and inquiry logs used throughout the learning unit can aid learners in using analytical skills to notice gaps in learning.

Generating Products for New Learning

All the inquiry process models take learners through create and share phases. There are many strategies and tools that can be used in "generating products that illustrate learning" (AASL 2018, Learner I.B.3.). Once learners have filled their knowledge gaps in their topic of study, it is important to provide learners some voice and choice in how they approach creating their new learning products. Research shows that when learners have some measure of control in their learning, feelings of self-worth and persistence in meeting the learning goals of the unit are engaged. This doesn't mean that learners have total control when using voice and choice. Balance is key. Depending on the scope and scale of the learning unit, and depending on the age level of the learner, products can be as simple as a timeline of the learner's life or as complex as a full presentation as part of a capstone project for high school seniors. Learners must consider the presentation tools (no-tech, low-tech, and high-tech) that can best help them illustrate that new learning has occurred. School librarians, as information specialists, can work with learners to consider the best way to organize their learning and to share it using the most appropriate medium possible. Learners will need to identify their audience and work through how their message illustrates that new learning has taken place.

Engaging Knowledge Creators

School librarians work to design learning experiences that aid learners in connecting prior knowledge to new knowledge, as well as creating context for this new learning by scaffolding lessons that allow those connections to take place. As information specialists, school librarians know about and share technologies that help learners create products that demonstrate new learning to an authentic audience. Because school librarians tend to be on the cutting edge of technology and resources, learners have an in-house guide through the Create Domain Competencies.

Questions for the Reflective Practitioner

1 What strategies do I use to help learners engage with prior knowledge and use evidence to investigate questions?

2 How can I work with classroom or content-area educators to scaffold learning experiences and help learners devise plans to fill knowledge gaps? What successful scaffolds are already in place?

3 What kinds of professional development can I offer my educator partners to foster collaborations that lead learners to create innovative learning products?

8

Fostering Problem Designers and Problem Solvers

EAM—Together Everyone Achieves More. This acronym is used often in team-building activities for both educators and learners, and it really is true. True teamwork allows the workload to be evenly distributed, provides opportunities to learn from diverse groups of people, and helps in goal setting, time management, and learning from each other. The instructional role the school librarian plays in developing and nurturing the learner to become proficient in the Shared Foundation of Inquire relies on how well the school librarian collaborates with other educators in designing learning experiences. Learning in today's schools has slowly shifted from high-stakes teaching-to-the-test back to a more-personalized, authentic learning approach. In the school library, learners become their own problem designers and problem solvers. The school library is uniquely suited to facilitate learners' engagement with knowledge-generating products that can have a real-world connection.

Probing to Gain New Knowledge

Using an inquiry research process model helps align the learner's path with the content learning outcomes. All the models presented in earlier chapters rely on learners using questions to help drive the inquiry process forward. School librarians also help move learners through the inquiry process by curating online pathfinders and resource shelves to help learners build on prior and background knowledge, using print and online scaffolds with learners to track their notes and learning, and collaboratively designing learning experiences that place the Competencies learners must develop in the context of the content area. The following techniques demonstrate ways of incorporating questioning in learning units and "ensuring that learners probe possible answers to questions" (AASL 2018, School Librarian I.B.1.). These questioning tools help learners develop questions that build on prior questions to dig deeper into learning. Use of learner-generated questions engages learners to *want* to know more because they asked the question! Getting learners to dig deeper encourages learners to create context to new meaning and builds metacognitive skills. Building in these opportunities throughout the learning unit provides learners multiple chances to practice this skill, thus allowing for transference to a new and different learning experience.

The school librarian and classroom educator can partner to create these questioning opportunities. The school librarian can use these learner-generated questions to help in the finding and evaluation of those resources. The classroom educator uses these learner-generated questions to check and aid the further development of content knowledge.

QFT

When using the QFT process with learners, it is very important to have the end in mind when developing the QFocus. "Designing the QFocus requires that you think about what students will be doing after they work on their questions" (Rothstein and Santana 2011, 34). When using the QFT to develop a "roadmap" for a learning unit, it is important to guide learners to where school librarians want them to go. In chapter 6, Jennifer Shaffer from Frederick County Public Schools in Walkersville, Maryland, used a picture of an alligator with baby alligators sitting on its head to talk about alligators and habitats of animals. Learners could then expand on what they learned about alligators and relate that learning to what humans need in order to survive. Engaging first with questions about the alligator and her babies allowed learners to naturally think like scientists. While using a nonfiction text about alligators to probe for answers to those questions, learners could also look for similarities to their own needs for survival in human habitats.

ESSENTIAL QUESTIONS

When creating Essential Questions for learners to work from in developing their own questions, educators should design each question so that the content becomes the answer and so that all learners see the value within the question and understand why are they working to answer the question. Tasks should be specifically designed so that the answers demonstrate learning (Wiggins and McTighe 2005, 121). For example, in chapter 4, the life science Essential Question "How can we prove that cells make up living things?" ties to content standards but is framed in such a way that learners have multiple starting points for investigating with their own questions. As learners move through the learning unit, school librarians can guide learners to resources that will help them make connections between their prior knowledge and new knowledge, thereby seeing the value of their questions and then working to find the answers.

NEED TO KNOW LIST

Like the QFocus and Essential Questions, questions developed on the Need to Know List from a PBL Driving Question need to be deliberate enough for learners to generate questions that have them probe for answers to gain the learning target(s) for the unit. An example of an elementary-level Driving Question might be this: "How can we design a playground that all students, no matter their size or ability, can use?" A secondary learner might encounter this question: "How do humans overcome prejudice and work toward social justice?"

After first working independently to develop their own questions, learners can work collaboratively to develop a class list of questions. This developed list can be done on chart paper or digitally in a simple shared document or in the class's learning management system. Keeping these lists visible in both the school library and the classroom will help the school librarian and educator to scaffold learning throughout the process so that all (or almost all) the answers are found.

K-W-L AND SEE, THINK, WONDER

K-W-L and See, Think, Wonder graphic organizers can be used throughout the learning unit and make great formative assessments for both the school librarian and the collaborating educator. These charts can be used to develop lessons, and resources can be curated based on what learners write on their charts. Over the course of the unit, learners will add to, take away from, and change the information probed for from the various resources provided during the unit.

Planning the perfect vacation is a topic both elementary and secondary learners can research. School librarians can start with pictures of different places that learners may not have visited before and use the See, Think, Wonder protocol to engage learners' curiosity about places to go for vacation. After this exercise, learners can move to using a K-W-L chart to engage learners' knowledge of vacations they have taken and thoughts about what would be the perfect vacation as well as what learners need to know in order to have that vacation. Learners can showcase what they learned about the "perfect vacation spot" by creating a travel brochure or slide presentation to persuade an authentic audience to take this vacation.

Planning for Knowledge Gaps

School librarians and classroom educators collaboratively design learning experiences related to content, using scaffolds to guide learners in refining their work by identifying and filling knowledge gaps. School librarians use inquiry process models to move learners into multiple learning opportunities to locate, access, use, reuse, and re-find resources. Through this process, learners are "devising and imple-menting a plan to fill knowledge gaps" (AASL 2018, School Librarian I.B.2.) as they synthesize their new learning into a product that will be shared with an audience. The following inquiry process models exhibit strategies and scaffolds that can be implemented to help learners find and close those learning gaps. These inquiry pro-cess models highlight the collaborative efforts of the school librarian and classroom educator when planning inquiry units to make sure learners are given resources and scaffolds to address and close these gaps.

GID

In the GID Create stage, learners get the opportunity to go beyond the factual learn-ing. This stage requires learners to dig deep and reflect to make connections to extend learning (Kuhlthau et al., 2012, 57). School librarians collaborate with other educators as a GID learning team to guide learners through this stage and push beyond simple facts to higher thinking skills. During this time, learners reflect on what they have assembled and consider what they have as a whole to determine what fits and what doesn't fit as learners see where connections can be made.

BIG6

In stages 4 and 5 of the Big6 model (Use of Information and Synthesis), learners work through both print and online resources to gain new knowledge and then organize and communicate their learning using the best vehicle. It is here that the school librarian can conference with learners, reviewing notes and findings to close learning gaps and help decide how best to showcase new learning.

STRIPLING MODEL OF INQUIRY

In the Express stage of the Stripling model, learners find connections between prior knowledge and new learning to create a product that demonstrates that learning. School librarians and classroom educators will help learners find the best format and method to showcase new learning that best fits an authentic audience's needs. In addition, school librarians help learners self-assess the learning process and the product developed (Stripling 2003, 16).

PATHWAYS TO KNOWLEDGE

In Pathways to Knowledge, learners move to the Communication stage. This stage takes learners through a process that teaches them to organize, apply, and present new knowledge relevant to learning outcomes for the unit. School librarians and classroom educators need to be careful to let learners create a product that illus-trates their learning. Learners need to understand that the information they found is new knowledge and that part of the learning involves the learners in applying and presenting that knowledge.

Developing Products for New Knowledge

Once learners have gathered all the resources used to probe their questions and have addressed and closed gaps in their learning, it is time for learners to consider products that will illustrate this new learning. School librarians need to connect with the collaborating educator at the beginning of the unit planning to discuss potential presentation modes and tools appropriate to the unit. This is an opportunity to suggest new technologies or presentation styles that could provide learners real-world applications of the content learning. Learners can use no-tech presentation tools, but there are also many free, online resources that can help learners put together presentations. However, as exciting as it is to incorporate new technologies or as comfortable as it is to assist learners using familiar modes and tools, learner voice and choice should prevail when "facilitating the development of products that illustrate learning" (AASL 2018, School Librarian I.B.3.).

All the inquiry process models state that when learners are at the stage of determining how to present their new learning, it is important for school librarians and their educator partners to allow learners to exercise voice and choice when deciding how to present their learning. This voice and choice will reveal the value in learners' unique capabilities and showcase hidden potential or talent in learners who might not be strong writers or able to organize information into a written format well. These learners may be better able to present information artistically or with technology.

Creating Creators

The role of the school librarian is to develop and encourage exploration and experimentation while engaging learners in an inquiry process. This function begins with school librarians and their collaborative partners designing inquiry units that teach learners how to ask good questions and probe resources for answers as they move through the inquiry unit. School librarians and educator partners also work to ensure that scaffolds are in place to support learners as they work to identify and close knowledge gaps. And last, school librarians and their educator partners provide a variety of means and modes that help learners express their new learning through the creation of products for an authentic audience. In this way, school librarians create learners who are problem designers and problem solvers and who achieve competency within the Inquire Create Domain.

Questions for the Reflective Practitioner

1 In what ways can I work with other educators and collaborate on learning units so that learners can experience success?

2 How can I help build scaffolds within lessons in the school library to help learners identify and close learning gaps?

3 How can I work with other educators to ensure that learners, through voice and choice, have an opportunity to be problem designers and problem solvers?

9

Creating in the School Library

hat is it about something not working that makes us want to fix it? Why won't the car start? How can we build a better bridge that has a positive impact on the environment? How can our commute be cut in half? Which American president deserves to be added to Mount Rushmore? How can we help those in our community who need the most help? The school library is the hub of problem designing and problem solving. School librarians work with all educators and learners in the school community, so it makes sense for the school library to be the epicenter of problem solving, tinkering, prototyping, and presenting information.

"The school library furthers learners' information-seeking and creative endeavors in an atmosphere that enables learners to wonder, explore, innovate, question, dabble, fail, invent, and reinvent" (AASL 2018, 72). To facilitate these learning experiences, the school library must provide opportunities and programs that support all learners using resources at their point of need.

Providing and Promoting Access

School librarians develop and maintain a wide variety of print and digital materials to facilitate teaching and learning. For school librarians to design collaborative learning experiences that enable new knowledge and support problem solving, the school library must offer "access to resources, information, ideas, and technology for all learners in the school community" (AASL 2018, School Library I.B.1.).

This mandate means that the school library, the school, or the district must have established collection development policies and procedures that include selection and reconsideration of materials within the school library collection. The school librarian should also have a budget and spending plan in line with these policies. These documents can also be used to advocate for learners, educators, and the school library collection with other stakeholders—administrators, school boards, parents—when additional resources are needed or when materials are questioned.

Remaining aware of curricular changes within the school and district, and at the state and national levels, is critical to planning and advocating for a dynamic school library collection that supports building information literacy skills through curriculum- and content-area-based experiences. Being part of the school's leadership team is a great way to stay informed about changes. Attending grade-level or subject-area meetings is another way to know what is happening in classrooms at the school. From these meetings, and other participation on district-level committees, the school librarian plans for and introduces resources that best support the curriculum and content areas for all stakeholders.

When working directly with other educators, "school librarians develop and facilitate learning activities that are academically rigorous, thought provoking, and inquiry-based. Integrating a collaborative approach across a variety of content areas, the school library promotes an inquiry process that includes posing questions, finding answers, and developing critical-thinking and communication skills through information exploration" (AASL 2018, 54). To effectively facilitate opportunities for collaborative instruction and implementation in which the school librarian and classroom educators can ensure that learners have access to and use a variety of resources, the school librarian must provide support through "digital and print information formats, mentors and experts, ideas, and technologies" (AASL 2018, 72).

The school library is an equalizer because all learners have access to its resources, so even if learners do not have access to technology at home, the school library "plays a crucial role in bridging digital and socioeconomic divides" (AASL 2018, 14). "Information technologies must be appropriately integrated and equitably available" (AASL 2018, 13). Working with other educators "to improve integration of learning technology into curriculum" (AASL 2018, 174) could be as simple as working with learners on using the online catalog to find books that meet their information need or as complex as using the library databases or using technology tools to keep track of notes and writing or to create and share new knowledge products.

School librarians also provide professional development for educator learners to showcase new resources that support curriculum goals and often share new technology tools that can help create blended learning experiences for learners. The AASL Best Websites and Best Apps for Teaching and Learning lists are a wonderful place to start when sharing new free or freemium technology tools used to enhance learning. Following tech groups such as @MindShiftKQED, @Eduporium, @OfficeofEdTech, and @TeachThought on social media can also provide a helpful aggregate of new educational technology tools and trends that school librarians can share with all learners.

Supporting Learners at the Point of Need

Through the school library, school librarians develop policies, procedures, programs, and services "to provide learner and educator access to staff and resources at the point of need" (AASL 2018, School Library I.B.2.). "The [school] library's physical space is conducive to learners' inquiry efforts because areas for collaboration and creation are provided. This learning environment necessitates a flexible schedule that ensures that learners and educators have access to both school library staff and resources" (AASL 2018, 72). To provide accessibility at the point of need on a fixed or flexible schedule, school librarians need to "be innovative inside the box," examining the realities within their learning communities and creating something new (Couros 2015, 36).

Extending hours before and after school, depending on the grade level of your learners, can help learners have access to staff and resources and a safe space to work or pursue personal interests while in the school building. If the school library has clerical staff or volunteers, open access to resources for learners and educators can continue even if the school librarian is busy teaching a class.

Creating an online presence is another way to extend services beyond the school day. Working with other educators to collaboratively create lessons and units that show learners how to access materials and resources using the school library's virtual tools while outside school creates independent lifelong learners. Use modules to address common library queries and post them to the school library's web page to provide learning opportunities 24/7 for all learners, including parents.

Most library management software provides ways for learners and educators to use school library resources without stepping into the library. Renewing items checked out and creating lists for requested resources that can be shared with the school librarian and populated by learners and other educators are just two online activities using library management software that won't require the school librarian to step away from instruction in order to facilitate. If formal software is not available, create a Google form that allows other educators to populate a list of titles or subjects needed that the school librarian can check each day. Set expectations for a turnaround time of twenty-four to forty-eight hours to keep the last-minute requests down. For learners, create an online survey whereby they can contribute to a wish list of titles to add to the collection. Collecting input from your consumers and collaborators in this way will also provide valuable data when advocating for your collection development budget.

Making school library resources easy to find, access, and use by all members of the school community allows school librarians to showcase how the school library plays an active role in learner growth. Using multiple avenues to showcase resources and ease of use is an important advocacy tool because it provides school librarians with data that can help in introducing new ideas to administrators and educator partners or in asking for increases to funding resources, services, or facilities.

Creating Success

The school library is the epicenter of the school. It is here that the resources, services, and instruction provided by the school librarian work to promote learners becoming problem designers and problem solvers. Working collaboratively with other educators, school librarians design and implement instruction that leads to the creation of new learning by learners in all content-area curriculums. By providing access to staff and resources 24/7, school librarians enable learners and educators to be self-sufficient and lifelong learners when it comes to "access to resources, information, ideas, and technology" (AASL 2018, School Library I.B.1.).

Questions for the Reflective Practitioner

1. What changes can I make to school library policies or procedures that will maximize learners' and educators' access to staff and resources?

2. How can I innovate inside the box to ensure that learners and educators feel that they are valued through school library practices, collections, and facilities?

3. What steps can I take to ensure that the school library enables generation of new knowledge through a wide variety of resources, information, and technology?

CREATE in Practice

reating a space of discovery and innovation is a goal of every educator. Often the largest classroom in the building, the school library is an ideal space for discovery and innovation. School librarians partner with other educators to create a learning space that melds content being taught with creativity and innovation for gaining and engaging knowledge as well as demonstrating new knowledge. In planning for instruction, school librarians can use or modify the strategies, tools, and example lessons included here. These examples incorporate the Competencies for the Inquire Create Domain in the learning unit. Through these lesson ideas, school librarians will see how to meet the Shared Foundation of Inquire through the Create Domain.

No-Tech Tools

Depending on the level of the learner and the type of new knowledge that needs to be presented, no-tech tools can be an easy, quick way to demonstrate learning. Written reports presented in a packet that documents how thinking unfolded throughout the inquiry process have been around since the report or research essay was born. Posters and trifold presentation boards are also inexpensive ways for learners to showcase products that illustrate learning. Three-dimensional models, timelines, and print formats create a visual for the audience and allow the learners to speak to their learning. Adding an oral component to these tools can extend the learners' Competencies and develop good verbal communication skills. Oral reports and dramatic or musical presentations also combine visual and auditory skills for learners to illustrate learning in a content area.

No-tech tools and communication strategies are affordable and time-tested classics for a reason and still serve a purpose. The following thinking routines are also as much a no-tech tool as the medium used to create the learning product. Thinking routines help learners organize their learning and distill the important and supporting elements of the message before sharing it through their chosen medium with others.

CONCEPT MAPS

Concept maps offer a nonlinear way for learners to connect knowledge through organizational thinking and provide a visual way to explain that early thinking to others. Using four steps, learners can map their understanding of a topic, concept, or issue.

> Step 1. *Generate* a list of ideas and initial thoughts that come to mind about this topic or issue.
>
> Step 2. *Sort* the ideas according to how central or tangential they are. Place central ideas near the center of the page and more-tangential ideas toward the outside of the page.
>
> Step 3. *Connect* the ideas by drawing lines between ideas that have something in common. Write a short sentence explaining how the ideas are connected.
>
> Step 4. *Elaborate* on any of the ideas or thoughts written so far by adding new ideas that expand, extend, or add to the initial ideas.

Learners can continue generating, connecting, and elaborating new ideas until there is a good representation of their understanding. This tool can also help learners identify gaps in their learning.

CONNECT-EXTEND-CHALLENGE

The Connect-Extend-Challenge routine helps learners make connections between new ideas and prior knowledge. It also encourages learners to take stock of ongoing questions, puzzles, and difficulties as they reflect on what they are learning.

> *Connect:* How are the ideas and information presented *connected* to what you already knew?
>
> *Extend:* What new ideas did you get that *extended* or pushed your thinking in new directions?
>
> *Challenge:* What is still *challenging* or confusing for you to get your mind around? What questions, wonderings, or puzzles do you now have?

The challenge questions lead learners to identify gaps in their learning and provide some direction for where and perhaps how to close those gaps (Ritchhart et al., 2011, 132).

THE 4 CS

The purpose of the 4 Cs visible thinking routine is to provide learners with a structure for discussion "built around making connections, asking questions, identifying key ideas, and considering applications . . . to help [learners] delve beneath the surface and go beyond first impressions" (Ritchhart et al., 2011, 140). This routine includes critical thinking but is not to be confused with the 4 Cs of critical thinking, creativity, communication, and collaboration.

> *Connections:* What connections do you draw between the text and your own life or your other learning?
>
> *Challenge:* What ideas, positions, or assumptions do you want to challenge or argue in the text?
>
> *Concepts:* What key concepts or ideas do you think are important and worth holding on to from the text?
>
> *Changes:* What changes in attitudes, thinking, or action are suggested by the text, either for you or others?

STOP, LOOK, LISTEN

The Stop, Look, Listen routine helps learners investigate truth claims and issues related to truth. It allows learners to stand back and think about ways to obtain information when trying to find out about the truth of something. Learners are encouraged to think critically about sources. This routine helps learners appreciate the deeper complexity of truth situations by addressing issues of bias and objectivity. These aspects are very important for older learners who are working through a pro/con or argumentative research inquiry.

The routine follows a simple three-step structure:

> *Stop:* Be clear about the claim. Define your question from your list of facts and uncertainties.
>
> *Look:* Find your sources. Where will you look? Consider obvious and nonobvious places.
>
> *Listen:* Hear with an open mind what the sources tell you.

Low-Tech Tools

Low-tech tools are easy-access tools that school librarians can use with learners to facilitate the development of products that illustrate learning. Most computers have several of these tools at the ready. If the school or district is using a 1:1 or if learners have access to a computer lab, using software commonly installed on most computers is an easy way for learners to create and share learning in the classroom, school, or global community. Many learners are already comfortable using presentation tools from Microsoft, Google, and

Apple. Other online tools including infographic creators and video sites offer good alternatives for learners who struggle with all-text representations of the learning.

GRAPHIC ORGANIZER TOOLS

Using draw or paint feature programs in common allows educators to create graphic organizers to help learners capture their thoughts and notes through an inquiry process. Microsoft Word provides templates and SmartArt that enable educators and learners to create graphic organizers. Learning management systems, if the school district uses one, also offer ways to organize learners' work that is already connected to the educator's class account.

PRESENTATION SOFTWARE

PowerPoint and Google Slides are two of the most common presentation tools and are simple to use. If the school district uses Apple products, the Keynote app is found on most devices running iOS. Providing instruction for learners on the elements and design of a good presentation is a useful extension lesson that works with most units.

DESIGN AND EDITING APPLICATIONS

Infographic tools like Canva, Piktochart, Infogram, and Google Charts offer opportunities for learners to create visual presentations. Other freemium online tools include Haiku Deck, Prezi, and Emaze, which allow learners to create presentations, website content, and other information styles. Flipgrid, Nearpod, Powtoon, Animaker, and Tellagami allow learners to create videos that can be shared with other learners.

 ## High-Tech Tools

High-tech tools provide opportunities for all learners to engage with technology to create demonstrations of new learning. These tools are a good option when the learning is going to be shared with a more-global audience because they are web-based and have features that enable sharing on the product platform. School districts or schools can subscribe to these tools for learners' use in generating products to illustrate learning. For those schools and districts that have a wide ability to innovate with technology, the following tools have been curated from the AASL Best Websites for Teaching and Learning annual recognition program.

SEESAW

The Seesaw platform allows learners to develop a digital portfolio of work that can be shared with the school librarian, the classroom educator, and other learners. Learners can take and upload photos and videos of work and can document thinking processes by including specific materials for the project.

TRELLO

The Trello platform allows learners to create boards and upload files from Google Drive, Dropbox, and OneDrive. For older learners, Trello can be used as a digital portfolio for the inquiry process. In addition, many school districts are working to create digital portfolios of learner growth through performance-based tasks. Seesaw and Trello can be digital storage spaces for these tasks.

BOOK CREATOR

Book Creator helps learners walk through the publishing world. Learners can include text, audio, video, and illustration. Many English language arts curriculum objectives have learners take a writing product all the way to the publication stage. Book Creator publishes learners' work online so learners can become real published authors.

BOOMWRITER

BoomWriter is another online publishing tool that aids learners who are collaborating on a writing assignment. This site is user friendly for younger learners as well as older learners. Like Book Creator, BoomWriter creates published authors. Both sites allow a global audience to see learners' work. Be sure to review privacy policies for sharing learners' work on such a scale.

KAPWING

Kapwing allows learners to create everything from video montages and memes to stop-action videos and sound effects. This tool is suited for older middle grades through adults and is especially useful for those learners who want to demonstrate their learning with visuals as opposed to or in addition to text. Kapwing is a good fit for those learners who express themselves better artistically than verbally.

Example Lesson Plans for Create

The following lesson plans promote content-area collaboration and are aligned to Create Domain Competencies. These lessons feature the options of no-tech, low-tech, and high-tech tools and can be adapted to meet the needs of your learners, educator partners, and school library environment.

REDUCE, REUSE, RECYCLE

Grade Levels: K–2

Contributor: Lori Donovan

Use this lesson for an Earth Day celebration to help younger learners realize their role in preserving and protecting Earth's resources. Extending the lesson with the art educator and STEAM educator (if your school has a STEAM program) can expand the lesson to involve the greater school community.

"I Can" Statement
I can reduce trash, reuse trash, and recycle trash into something new.

AASL Standards Framework for Learners
I.B.3. Learners engage with new knowledge by following a process that includes generating products that illustrate learning.

Content Areas
Science/STEM/STEAM

Duration
Two 45-minute class sessions

Materials
- *Amazing Recycled Projects You Can Create* by Marne Ventura
- *Curious George Discovers Recycling* by Erica Zappy
- Plastic bottles, aluminum cans, coffee cans, soda tabs, rubber bands, glue, scissors, and the like.

Lesson
Before: Set up a trash area in the school library. Have learners talk about what happens to areas that are covered in trash. Ask learners, "How do we clean up the mess? How can we make the school library a cleaner place? What other areas in the school do you think could be cleaned up and why?"

During: Read *Curious George Discovers Recycling* by Erica Zappy aloud to learners. Ask learners what George learned about recycling and what they can do to help recycle items. Share with the class the nonfiction book *Amazing Recycled Projects You Can Create* by Marne Ventura. Other titles that support reduce, reuse, and recycle themes can be used if these titles are not available. After reading and discussing these books, ask learners to help gather the trash in the school library and reuse the materials to create a recycled project. Display learners' recycled projects in the school library to encourage others to recycle.

Assessment: Assess learners on an oral or written component in which they describe how their project reduced and reused trash and recycled it into a product that can be used by themselves or by someone else. Alternatively, or in addition, ask learners to develop a list of suggestions for reducing, reusing, and recycling materials that can be posted around the school and community and assess them on this list.

USING NONFICTION TEXT FEATURES

Contributor: Lori Donovan

Nonfiction text features allow learners to quickly access information to answer a research or inquiry question. In this lesson learners will see and access both print and digital nonfiction resources to answer topic questions.

"I Can" Statement

I can use nonfiction text features to preview a reading selection.

AASL Standards Framework for Learners

I.B.1. Learners engage with new knowledge by following a process that includes using evidence to investigate questions.

Content Area

Language Arts

Duration

One 45-minute class session

Materials

- A variety of nonfiction texts that contain these nonfiction features: bold words, captions, photographs, maps, and graphs
- Library databases to access digital nonfiction resources
- Question sheets at each station

Lesson

Before: Ask learners about the difference between fiction and nonfiction texts. Ask learners what features or elements are likely to be seen in nonfiction texts. Responses might include bold words, captions, photographs, maps, and graphs. Showcase pages copied from a nonfiction title. As learners identify the nonfiction features, circle or highlight the elements. Repeat this exercise with a library database.

During: Ask learners to explore three stations containing different types of nonfiction resources. At each station learners will respond to questions using the nonfiction text provided. The question sheets will vary depending on the resources and topics featured at the stations. After visiting three stations, learners will select and check out books featured at the stations. After checkout, as a class, learners can compare answers to questions at the stations they visited. If there isn't time, this can be the opening review activity the next time the class visits the school library. For an extension lesson, discuss the differences between fiction and nonfiction titles.

Assessment: Use the question sheets from the stations to assess how well learners used the nonfiction text features to answer the questions about the resource topics. Alternatively, assess oral or written explanations from learners about how they were able to find the answer based on the text feature used.

JUST THE RIGHT PET FOR ME!

Grade Levels: 3–5

Contributors: Heather Hess, Caroline Romano, Rita Saylor, Sue Strada, and Donald Walutes

This lesson is a continuation of the *Should a Tiger Be a Pet?* lesson presented in part II and extends the theme of finding the right pet for learners' families. Because learners already determined that tigers are not good pets, this inquiry allows learners to research different kinds of pets and to make a new selection. Learners will write a persuasive letter to their parents asking for the pet they researched and explaining why the pet would be a good fit for their family.

"I Can" Statement

I can follow an inquiry process to answer my research question.

AASL Standards Framework for Learners

I.B.1. Learners engage with new knowledge by following a process that includes using evidence to investigate questions.

I.B.2. Learners engage with new knowledge by following a process that includes devising and implementing a plan to fill knowledge gaps.

I.B.3. Learners engage with new knowledge by following a process that includes generating products that illustrate learning.

Content Areas

Language Arts
Science/STEM/STEAM

Duration

Three to four 45-minute class sessions

Materials

- *How Do Dinosaurs Choose Their Pets?* by Jane Yolen
- *The Perfect Pet* by Margie Palatini
- *The One and Only Ivan* by Katherine Applegate
- Keeping and Caring for Your Pet series from Enslow Publishing
- *Oh, the Pets You Can Get! All about Our Animal Friends* by Tish Rabe

- Animal websites curated through KidSites.com
- Library databases

Lesson

Before: Remind learners of the previous activity about whether tigers make good pets. Explain that because the class decided, based on evidence annotated in NoodleTools, that tigers are not good house pets, learners will now research what kind of pet best fits their family's lifestyle.

During: Ask learners the following questions as they begin their research:

- "How would you gather information if you wanted to convince your family to get a pet?"
- "What animal would you like to research, and what do you already know about this type of animal?"
- "What else do you want or need to know about owning this pet?"
- "Who would you talk to or where would you go to find more answers about pet care for this animal?"
- "Where in the school library would you find information to answer your questions?"

Learners will use the resources curated at tables and on the computer to find information about the animal or animals chosen and determine which pet is the best for their family. Learners will compose a persuasive letter to convince their families that they would be great pet owners. Learners should include details that specifically identify the pet they have chosen, their responsibilities to that pet, and how caring for a pet will benefit the family. As an extension activity, invite a panel of animal care professionals to speak with the class in person or in a virtual setting. Local business professionals or organizations to consider may include dog groomers, veterinary professionals, pet supply business owners, breeders, pet walkers, animal trainers, zookeepers, 4-H leaders, and local wildlife organization representatives. Learners should generate at least two questions to ask invited speakers about their careers.

Assessment: Develop a rubric to assess learners' persuasive letters to their families. Share this rubric with learners as they get started to help them identify the critical elements of organizing and writing a persuasive letter. If learners interview people in the career field, assess learners' interview questions.

CIVIL WAR BIOGRAPHIES

Grade Levels: 3–5

Contributor: Julie Trammell-McGill

This lesson helps learners understand famous people from the Civil War. Learners will explore famous people who were influential at the time. During the inquiry unit, learners will research information and then write a persuasive two- to three-paragraph essay about a person of their choice from this time. They will then present their project to their peers.

"I Can" Statement

I can explain why my chosen person was influential in the Civil War.

AASL Standards Framework for Learners

I.B.1. Learners engage with new knowledge by following a process that includes using evidence to investigate questions.

I.B.2. Learners engage with new knowledge by following a process that includes devising and implementing a plan to fill knowledge gaps.

I.B.3. Learners engage with new knowledge by following a process that includes generating products that illustrate learning.

Content Areas

History/Social Science
Language Arts

Duration

Three 45-minute class sessions

Materials

- Library databases
- List of influential figures from the Civil War
- Pathfinder with guidelines, rubric, and resources (www.livebinders.com/play/play?id=2230342)

Lesson

Before: Following instruction from the classroom educator on the events of the Civil War, ask learners, "Who were the people behind the Civil War?" Have learners tell a classmate what they think or know.

During: Provide a list of influential Civil War figures and ask each learner to select one figure to research and write about. Assign learners to write a two- to three-paragraph biography of an influential Civil War figure. Allow learners to work independently but be prepared to offer support as needed. At the completion of the assignment, ask learners to present their biography to the class.

Assessment: Assess learners on their knowledge of the Civil War's famous people. Assessment rubrics for biographies and oral communication are freely available online. Also, provide opportunities for peer feedback about the presentations.

DIAGNOSING DISEASE

Grade Levels: 6–8

Contributors: Gretchen Hazlin, Susanna Carey, and Brandon Filsinger

Developed collaboratively between the school librarian and the health and physical education chair, this lesson is an effort to get away from the dull disease research presentations. Learners become medical residents, diagnosing the diseases of volunteer patients.

"I Can" Statement

I can understand causes and symptoms of a variety of diseases (along with preventive strategies) so that I am able to live my best life.

AASL Standards Framework for Learners

I.B.1. Learners engage with new knowledge by following a process that includes using evidence to investigate questions.

I.B.2. Learners engage with new knowledge by following a process that includes devising and implementing a plan to fill knowledge gaps.

Content Areas

Health/Physical Education

Duration

Three 45-minute class sessions

Materials

- Kilmer Medical Center (kilmermed.weebly.com): This website is the anchor resource for this lesson. It features information on diseases, vital signs, and treatments.

Lesson

Before: Introduce learners to the lesson with a short video from real-world medical professionals, sharing about patient care, diagnosing patients, and bedside manner.

During: Set up a classroom or lecture hall as a medical center with eight exam rooms. Use folding gym mats to create the rooms and place a chair in each room for the patient. Give patient volunteers a list of symptoms to exhibit. Patients start by sharing their age, gender, and the top symptom listed. Learners will act as medical residents attempting to figure out the rest of the patient's symptoms by asking questions. Patients will answer questions with primarily yes or no responses. Using the Kilmer Medical Center anchor website, learners will rule out various conditions and then return to the patient to investigate further. Once the learner medical residents diagnose the patient and confirm the diagnosis with the school librarian and classroom educator, learners will present the diagnosis to the patient. After diagnosing the patient, learners will access the Treatments page of the Kilmer Med website to collaboratively develop a treatment plan for their patient and create a poster-sized organizer to share their findings. Display the finished posters in the library so learners can circulate in a "treatment rounds" Gallery Walk and learn from each other.

Assessment: Assess learners on how well they communicated with the patient and on their inquiry skills to "diagnose" the illness that learners researched. During the inquiry process, asking the right question of the patient and with purpose demonstrates that learners understand that the types of questions asked lead to specific types of answers.

FAMOUS AMERICANS ON SOCIAL MEDIA

Grade Levels: 9–12

Contributor: Lori Donovan

Learners are provided voice and choice in choosing a famous American to research, given lots of freedom in expressing their social media posts, and encouraged to be creative in their demonstration of knowledge of their person. Learners will share their social media templates with the school librarian and classroom educator through a Google platform.

"I Can" Statement

I can demonstrate understandings of contributions of famous Americans through social media outlets.

AASL Standards Framework for Learners

I.B.3. Learners engage with new knowledge by following a process that includes generating products that illustrate learning.

Content Areas
History/Social Science
Language Arts

Duration
Three 90-minute class sessions

Materials
- Chromebooks
- Google Drive/Slides social media profile template (https://www.educators technology.com/2013/03/3-awesome-facebook-templates-for-your.html)
- Library databases
- Library of Congress: American Memory
- Library of Congress: American Memory Timeline

Lesson

Before: Instruct learners to choose one famous American studied in U.S. history to research and then develop a social media presence for that person.

During: Using the library databases and history websites, learners will gather interesting facts about their famous person, including the person's friends and enemies, in order to create a realistic social media presence for the historical person. Ask learners to create a Works Cited page to reflect their research. Provide learners with the social media template to create the famous Americans' social media pages. Both ReadWriteThink and the blog *Educational Technology and Mobile Learning* provide editable Facebook-like templates for learner use. Ask learners to create a thread of social media posts reflecting their knowledge and understanding of their famous American, including interactions with at least three other historical figures whom their American would have known personally.

Assessment: Assess learners using a multimedia rubric on how accurately the famous American was represented on social media. Research skills can be analyzed informally through exit tickets and a Works Cited list attached to the social media template used.

GLOBAL GOALS FROM MULTIPLE PERSPECTIVES

Grade Levels: 9–12

Contributor: Lori Donovan

This collaborative project involves a service-learning component using the United Nations Global Goals. Learners evaluate a real-world problem or social issue by looking at it from multiple perspectives. This project engages learners as they work together to create a capstone or service-learning project to meet one of the UN Global Goals.

"I Can" Statement

I can look at a social issue from multiple perspectives and articulate them in writing to form a conclusion.

AASL Standards Framework for Learners

I.B.1. Learners engage with new knowledge by following a process that includes using evidence to investigate questions.

Content Areas

Language Arts
Science
History/Social Studies

Duration

Seven to eight 90-minute class sessions

Materials

- Chromebooks
- United Nations Global Goals website
- Inquiry log for each perspective
- Nonfiction print resources
- Library databases
- Websites of nonprofits that support the global goals

Lesson

Before: Ask learners to use the UN Global Goals website to choose a social issue to research in developing a service-learning project. Learners should look at multiple sides of the issue to design a project that addresses as many perspectives as possible.

During: Learners will research the selected global goal from a variety of perspectives using school library resources. Explaining the topic from all points of view, learners will write an essay drawing a conclusion about which point of view could meet the global goal in the timeliest manner. After consulting with the school librarian and classroom educator, learners will combine similar global goals and develop service-learning project ideas. In groups, learners will develop project proposals and present their ideas to local community outreach organizations. After presenting their ideas to local charities, learners will work with the agencies to develop and run the service-learning projects.

Assessment: Assess learners' research skills and information literacy. The educator partner will assess content literacy. Gaps in learning and the final products can be assessed by both the school librarian and the classroom educator.

PART IV

Share

10

Collaborating with Learning

aking pride in accomplishments, especially ones gained after trying to succeed multiple times or practicing many hours, is something that we all do. Professional athletes, actors, dancers, and singers who make their talent look easy inspire others to do the same. In school, this is also true. Learners feel great pride when they accomplish something; new learning, finally understanding something that wasn't making sense, is something to celebrate. School librarians and other educators collaborate to create learning units that allow learners to persevere through the inquiry process, achieve success, and demonstrate new learning to a larger community.

In the Inquire Share Domain, learners will be using an inquiry-based process to adapt, communicate, and exchange ideas and products presented by themselves and others in the learning cycle (AASL 2018, Learner I.C.). During this process, learners will know that they are in "a safe, accepting, and open environment that supports personal growth, confidence, critical comment, and constructive praise" and that "learners interact with and provide constructive feedback on many formats of other learners' content" (AASL 2018, 70). Within this framework learners learn how to provide constructive feedback, act on the feedback to improve, and share products with an authentic audience.

Interacting with Content

Many learners, no matter how well they read and comprehend information, have difficulty knowing what information is important to use in answering their research questions. It is important for learners to be able to "[interact] with content presented by others" (AASL 2018, Learner I.C.1.) so that learners can incorporate direct quotations, paraphrases, and summaries to draw conclusions that answer their research questions. Working with classroom and content educators, school librarians design lessons that show learners how to read to learn, pull out relevant information that helps answer the research questions, and apply those answers to new learning. Through modeling, the school librarian can scaffold learners to understand how to pull information into new learning.

All the inquiry process models include ideas for enabling learners to discern what information is needed and how it must be stated. Journaling and creating inquiry logs aid learners in understanding and reflecting on the information they collect to determine what will be used in the final product. Graphic organizers and charts (both print and digital) can be used after learners have determined what information will be used and can now organize and synthesize the information into what will become a final product. These tools also will help learners know when they have enough information to answer their research question, or if they will need to fill in gaps where information is missing or incomplete.

Once learners can see what information they will use in their final products, the school librarian reminds (or reteaches) learners about the ethical use of integrated content presented by others in the creation of new knowledge and products. Depending on the age of the learner, methods for delivering these lessons will vary. These lessons should be embedded into the chosen inquiry-based learning process model to allow for full understanding of not only the what and the how but also the why. Many online resources are available to help school librarians best facilitate lessons on ethical use, such as Common Sense Media, Google for Education, NetSmartz, and Microsoft Education.

Each of the inquiry process models aids in the ethical use of information in much the same way, with the emphasis on learners' need to understand that although using integrated content presented by others is a democratic right, it comes with responsibilities as a citizen.

Guided Inquiry builds on learners' "understanding of the value of an author's work." In the Create and Share phases, learners learn the importance of citing and the types of information that should be included (Kuhlthau et al., 2012, 93). Understanding use of content presented by others strengthens learners' content knowledge and provides context to knowledge. Part of that learning is the ethical integration of that content into new learning products.

In stage 4 of the Big6 protocol, learners engage with the text (reading, listening, and viewing) and then use important information from that text. When learners "locate sources and find appropriate information, they must be able to read and understand, or listen effectively, or watch for key concepts and examples relevant to their task. Otherwise, the source will not help meet their information need" (Eisenberg and Berkowitz 2000, 23).

In the Express stage of the Stripling model, learners "apply understandings to a new context, new situation—create a product to demonstrate new understanding." Learners then work through a writers' workshop stance to determine how best to communicate their main and supporting points in the product and "evaluate and revise [their] own product based on self-assessment and feedback from others" (Stripling 2003, 16).

In the Pathways to Knowledge protocol, "when students have gathered information and constructed new knowledge, their next step is to apply that knowledge in some manner." Learners must have voice and choice when putting this knowledge together into a presentation format (Pappas and Tepe 2002, 20).

School librarians can help learners by offering mini-lessons about using the context of the information found to decide which sources will best help learners make connections between new knowledge and prior knowledge. Lessons about citation of sources also will assist learners. In addition, school librarians can aid learners by having them put information into graphic organizers, by conferencing with learners and peers, and by introducing learner self-reflection on the process and the product design.

All the inquiry process models stress the importance of allowing learners to have voice and choice in how they present their new knowledge. School librarians need to delve into their own toolbox to find the method of product development that best serves the inquiry process product. District-wide professional development on presentation styles and types is most helpful for all educators, and school librarians can be leaders in this type of professional development.

Providing Constructive Feedback

Learners thrive in a culture that encourages them to exchange specific, kind, helpful, and constructive feedback with other learners. This skill needs to be taught so that learners see that learning is a process and understand that "providing constructive feedback" will help them and their peers improve (AASL 2018, Learner I.C.2.). Feedback should be given by the school librarian and classroom educator as well as by peers. Research shows that constructive feedback enhances learner success and improves learner achievement.

The skills of communicating feedback constructively must be modeled in the classroom and school library. Ron Berger's *Austin's Butterfly* feedback lesson walks learners of different ages through Austin's drafts of a butterfly drawing and talks about offering peer critique and using multiple drafts to create a final product. ReadWriteThink has a lesson that walks learners through a peer review process to help learners improve their writing and communication skills. The blog *MindShift* has tips for preparing learners to give feedback to each other (Schwartz 2017).

Using the Gallery Walk strategy in the beginning stages of the inquiry process allows feedback from peers and educators to help learners reframe their direction or continue moving forward. "This discussion technique allows students to be actively engaged as they walk throughout the classroom. They work together in small groups to share ideas and respond to meaningful questions, documents, images, problem-solving situations or texts" ("Gallery Walk," n.d.). Alternatively, this technique done in silence allows learners to process ideas and write short, specific feedback based on what the presenter wishes for feedback.

For writing, using the strategy Two Stars and a Wish teaches learners to find two things they like about what was written and to express a wish for clarification of or changes to the writing. Checklists and rubrics can also be used when teaching learners how to give and receive feedback. There are many ways in which learners can learn how to give specific, kind, helpful, constructive feedback. Practicing this skill often best prepares learners not only to give feedback but to act upon the feedback they receive as well.

Acting on Feedback

For feedback to be effective and received well, the school librarian and classroom educator need to establish an environment that is conducive to giving and receiving feedback. "The feedback process empowers each learner to grow and to improve his or her own learning and be accountable for knowledge products demonstrating that learning" (AASL 2018, 70). Routines need to be developed at the beginning of the year and referred to often to help establish a culture that supports "acting on feedback to improve" (AASL 2018, Learner I.C.3.).

Classbuilding "provides mutual support among all the students in a class and creates a positive context for learning" (Kagan and Kagan 2015, 9.1). As part of building Third Space theory, class members need to know that they are part of a large learning community and that working together will build trust and support to maximize learning in both the classroom and the school library.

TeachThought offers five simple social-emotional learning strategies that school librarians can use to help create a culture in which feedback can be given and received well so that acting on that feedback leads to improvement:

- Mindfulness: Paying attention not only to those learners around them but to themselves as well creates an awareness that leads to a more-harmonious classroom.
- Challenge Thinking: Learners who can learn from mistakes and move forward are more successful than those who cannot.
- Persistence and Determination: Some learners adapt to this more naturally than others. Coaching learners is key.
- Empathy: Teaching learners how to be empathetic will build an awareness of others that will make divergent thinking easier for learners to master.

- Gratitude: Incorporating gratitude lessons within learning experiences provides learners opportunities to learn and appreciate gratitude among themselves and others (TeachThought Staff 2018).

Sharing New Knowledge

Once the feedback cycle has concluded, and learners have addressed all the gaps in their learning during the inquiry process, it is time for them to think about "sharing [their new learning] with an authentic audience" (AASL 2018, Learner I.C.4.). Use the district's policy on sharing learner work more globally to help guide how learners share new knowledge. If the district has an internal server that learners can share, start there. If the district's policy allows learner work to be shared to a wider audience, using technology presentation tools is helpful. Google, Microsoft, and Apple provide many presentation tools that are free to use on their platforms. Some freemium technology tools that can be used include Prezi, Haiku Deck, Glogster, and Pear Deck.

For learners to understand relevance to learning, connecting new knowledge to real-world applications is key when planning inquiry projects with educator partners. Research demonstrates that when learners are more engaged, the learning is longer lasting and more-easily transferable to new situations. Providing learners more voice and choice in how they create and share their new knowledge also has been shown to support these transferable skills.

Questions for the Reflective Practitioner

1 Why is it important for all learners to be self-reflective, not only at the end of a learning process but throughout the process?

2 How can I best plan to allow for reflection for myself, my instructional partners, and my learners?

3 In what ways can I promote the practice of sharing learning so that learners feel confident? In what ways can I encourage persistence throughout the inquiry process?

11

Sharing Success

othing brings an educator more joy than seeing a learner accomplish a task. It is even more eventful if that learner really struggled with the task before the light bulb "switched on" in the learner's brain. "School librarians help learners feel confident and encourage their persistence throughout inquiry" (AASL 2018, 71). Establishing a culture in which it is safe to fail forward and which includes scaffolds from the school librarian to help build stamina for learning, even when it goes wrong, allows learners to develop the habit of moving forward even when faced with obstacles and difficulties. These skills will be beneficial as learners move beyond a K–12 environment into college and career life. School librarians and their educator partners work collaboratively to develop learning experiences through which learners have the opportunity to develop this stamina and create learning products that the learners are proud to share with others.

School librarians guide learners in maintaining focus throughout the inquiry process with an emphasis not only on content learning but also on the 4 Cs—critical thinking, creativity, communication, and collaboration. School librarians will develop a culture that fosters inquiry through "collaborative encounters that promote constructive, honest, and reflective feedback as well as unique, authentic opportunities to share learning" (AASL 2018, 71–72). The inquiry process models used throughout this book highlight this feature as a structure that guides learners as they work through the inquiry project.

With Third Space theory in Guided Inquiry, school librarians "engage students in ways that matter in their lives and enable them to contribute experiences and outside-of-school mergers that promote intellectual inquiry, deepen learning, and meet curriculum goals" (Kuhlthau et al., 2015, 27). Connecting learning to the real world gives learners an opportunity to make connections between learning and application, giving the why to learning. These experiences also allow learners to tap into their natural interests and think of life beyond a K–12 environment.

In stages 4 and 5 of the Big6 method, learners use skills to extract and synthesize information. Connections to prior knowledge are taking place in these stages along with the building of new knowledge. The school librarian works with other educators to scaffold learners to make connections with this new knowledge, to make real-world connections, and to allow for transference of knowledge. Transference, when practiced throughout the learners' time in the K–12 environment, will help learners make connections to content and the real world more often and more easily.

During the Construct and Express stages of the Stripling model, learners are thinking deeply about the new information to "test predictions and hypotheses, to recognize authors' points of view and consider alternative perspectives, and to construct new and appropriate knowledge based on evidence" (Stripling 2003, 15). Through trial and error, learners learn how they will be expected to work in the real world. No one in a real-world job environment is asked to show knowledge by taking a test.

Pappas and Tepe (2002) described the Interpretation and Communication stages in the Pathways to Knowledge model as the time when learners are working to construct new knowledge in ways that best communicate that new learning. Providing voice and choice in this presentation of new knowledge gives learners a real-world experience of life in a job or career.

In addition, building scaffolds in learning experiences helps learner fail forward fast to build the disposition to persevere. Learners develop the persistence to move forward when stumbles in learning happen. Through collaboration, the school librarian and educator partners work to aid learners in developing those skills needed to interpret information and to best communicate learning that best meets the needs of the intended audience.

Assessing Focus within Inquiry

"Formative assessment provides school librarians with feedback about their instruction; . . . [and] permits school librarians to make adjustments, tweaking their practice at every juncture of a lesson" (AASL 2018, 151). When school librarians are collaboratively planning with educator partners on an inquiry project, it is important to have a discussion about "assisting in assessing the inquiry-based research process" (AASL 2018, School Librarian I.C.1.). These discussions should include who will be assessing learners along the way, how they will be assessing learners, and what will be assessed.

School librarians are content specialists on information literacy. For the Inquire Shared Foundation, school librarians can assess learners on their ability to formulate inquiry questions based on an interest and/or a curricular need or on how well they follow an inquiry process from start to finish. Learners can also be assessed on their abilities to locate, access, and use information ethically and responsibly. Last, learners can be assessed on how well they are able to determine the best method to share their new knowledge. Classroom educators are content-level experts and should be assessing how learners use their prior knowledge and apply new knowledge to demonstrate the learning goals of the content area.

In GID, three concepts of information literacy can be assessed: "How information is organized; how it promotes curiosity, reflection, and enlightenment; and [how] interpreting information over time leads to deep learning" (Kuhlthau et al., 2015, 74–76). The assessment of these additional soft skills measures growth in learners' metacognitive skills. Keeping an inquiry journal and using graphic organizers can aid in self-reflection for learners.

In the Big6 model, assessment should be done "in [the] context of real curriculum needs" both formatively and summatively. However, Eisenberg and Berkowitz (2014) also stressed that assessment must include the process as well as the product. This means that learners must be able not only to complete the task but also to articulate the process they used to complete the task and transfer that learning to a new inquiry unit.

Barbara Stripling stated, "Assessment involves looking at the learning throughout the learning experience before, during, and after" (Stripling 2003, 31). Stripling also stressed that these assessments must be authentic and measure the inquiry process as well as the product. If learning is a process, then assessments designed by the school librarian and classroom educator need to reflect that process to help ensure learner success.

And the Pathways to Knowledge framework focuses assessments on both product and process in an authentic manner. As technology has moved forward, giving learners more choice in how knowledge is created, it is important to have assessments built around process and product (Pappas and Tepe 2002, 97).

Both school librarians and classroom educators bring levels of expertise to a learning unit. Building on each other's strengths when "assisting in assessing the inquiry-based research process" brings a much richer learning experience to the learner (AASL 2018, School Librarian, I.C.1.).

Sharing and Reflecting on Products

When it comes to learners sharing their new knowledge, it is important to have a space (both physical and virtual) "to share learning products and reflect on the learning process" with a wider community (AASL 2018, School Librarian I.C.2.). School libraries are great physical spaces in which learners can share their learning with their school community, and school libraries provide a low-cost way to present displays that will draw learners and other educators into the school library. A digital learning commons on the school library website is one way learners can share their learning, as well as request and provide feedback on their and others' work. This digital learning commons can be internally linked through a learning management system or, if the district allows, can be done on the open side of the school library website.

Reflecting on the process with others should include learners, not just the educator and school librarian. Working with learners to evaluate the process and the product through self-reflection aids learners in developing the metacognitive skills needed to learn how to learn and how to manage that learning in ways that best serve each learner. Inquiry journals and logs aid learners (and school librarians and classroom educators) in reflecting on learning. Rubrics and checklists also help with formative assessments to guide instruction throughout the inquiry process.

Conferencing with learners throughout the inquiry process is also a way to help learners reflect on the process and product. One goal should be how to improve or make changes in what was done to help learners identify when persistence was needed and why. Questions such as "What did you learn?" and "What would you do differently?" and "What will you do differently next time?" celebrate the learning process even when learners are met with roadblocks or mistakes. Through conferences with the school librarian and classroom educator, learners can develop an action plan to help avoid the mistakes made in this inquiry process and proceed forward with fewer stumbling blocks the next time. These conversations also aid the educator and school librarian when reflecting on the inquiry project itself—what went well, what parts needed more scaffolding for learners, and what adjustments need to be made for this inquiry project or other collaborative work.

Assessment and the sharing of knowledge based on that assessment are important to model in an inquiry project for learners. Such modeling scaffolds lifelong learning skills as well as the soft skills needed in a post-K–12 environment.

Questions for the Reflective Practitioner

1. What are the best assessment scaffolds I can use to keep the excitement in learning, even when learners encounter roadblocks?

2. How can self-reflection enable learners to build the stamina needed to continue to Inquire throughout the inquiry unit?

3. In what ways can I model persistence during an inquiry unit, especially when working with learners who don't often find success at school?

12

Showcasing Learning
in the School Library

S **mall children are so excited when they share what they** have done—from the smallest of scribbles displayed with honor on the refrigerator to shouting when they win a small prize. Educators and school librarians need to encourage that excitement and joy in learning, especially when it comes to learners sharing their learning with their community and beyond. The school library space is universal—all are welcome to physically be in the space and to have their ideas heard and respected, even if those ideas differ from others' ideas; this acceptance can then spread throughout the building. In the school library, learners and educator partners will find equitable access to physical and digital spaces so that learner outcomes are positively impacted.

The school library is an "inviting, flexible, and safe [place that] helps learners develop important dispositions, including acceptance, encouragement, and understanding. Learners develop trust and thrive in an effective school library that gives them freedom to move through the inquiry process in a barrier-free, universally designed environment that allows equitable physical and intellectual access" (AASL 2018, 73). All the inquiry process models discussed in this book stress that this disposition must be in place for any learning to take place. "School librarians tailor learning outcomes to standards and all learner levels, and communicate these targets clearly in the school library space" (AASL 2018, 73). Making these outcomes clear shows learners that the school library and school librarian are partners with them in their development and sharing of new knowledge gained for personal and academic pursuits.

Inquiry within the Learning Environment

Because the school library is a space that the whole school community accesses, it is important that the school librarian creates a space that the whole school community wants to use. Having an open-door policy when the school building is open that is flexible in its schedule to allow access to materials at the point of need, even if the school librarian is not available, is important in establishing that all are welcome. Having a learning environment that is "inviting, safe, [and] adaptable" for large groups, small groups, or individuals is also important for making the space "conducive to learning" (AASL 2018, School Library I.C.1.). Making sure that the library's physical space complies with the universal design requirements of the Americans with Disabilities Act ensures that all users have access to the space. Having a variety of flexible seating options can help address the different ways in which learners learn and makes them feel comfortable in the space, allowing deeper learning to happen.

Physical teaching spaces in the school library need to have vantage points so all learners can see and hear the lesson in progress. Most school libraries are now equipped with presentation tools such as Smart Boards or Promethean Boards, wireless monitors with touchscreens that allow for movement while instruction is taking place. Even some tables now house small presentation screens that users can plug into for sharing information in small groups. No-tech tools like white boards, and walls and furniture that have dry-erase paint applied, can also assist instruction for large or small groups.

Beyond the physical space, the school library should also maintain a virtual presence so that learners and educator partners have 24/7 access to library resources. Putting modules on the school library website with quick videos explaining how to do searches in the online catalog or the library databases will empower users to follow through to find what they are looking for on their own. Providing modules about how to put books on hold or creating a list of books needed to teach a lesson will support educators and learners alike. Putting resources about copyright and fair use on the website will remind users about applicable laws and ethical use of information. Other resources that aid learners and educators, such as open educational resources (OER) and other quality resources available on the free web, should be included on the school library website as well.

Providing Barrier-Free Learning Environments

In addition to the physical space being equitable for learning opportunities, the school library must be a space that allows learners and educators to access information barrier-free at their point of need (AASL 2018, School Library I.C.2.). Flexible scheduling is the most ideal, but school librarians can work with clerical staff and volunteers to aid in finding and checking out resources while the school librarian is busy collaborating with educators and working with learners. Trusted older student learners (if your district allows) can also help with checking materials in and out and even shelving them so that popular items can quickly be checked out again. The physical space needs to be flexible in design so that a whole class, a small group, or individuals can work simultaneously with minimal distraction or disruption.

The school library's virtual space also must be flexible to accommodate the needs of all learners before, during, and after school hours. Designing a website so that learners who are auditorily or visually impaired, learners whose native language isn't English, or learners who struggle with using technology can all access and use the site for their learning needs is just as important as the placement of the furniture and resources in the physical space. When using technology during instruction, making sure that all learners can access the technology and can follow along is important in building the stamina and persistence needed when gaining new knowledge.

Using Data to Support Inquiry Learning

As part of modeling self-reflection, school librarians need to take note of how learners and educators are using the resources provided by the school library. This process includes looking at data such as circulation statistics, collection analysis, and collection mapping tools to measure whether the school library is meeting learners' and educators' personal and academic needs and to "improve resources, instruction, and services" (AASL 2018, School Library I.C.3.).

The school librarian constantly consults professional journals on both school library and educational pedagogy to review best practices in educational trends to improve teaching and learning. Attending conferences and workshops held by library associations and other educational groups locally and at the state and national levels is another way to "improve resources, instruction, and services" (AASL 2018, School Library I.C.3.). Developing a professional learning community within the district is a way to share struggles and triumphs and provides a cohort to help plan new inquiry projects that can be done in the school library or collaboratively with educator partners. Social media are also great for developing a professional learning network that extends beyond the locality, and membership in professional organizations can help school librarians be reflective about improving their practice.

Creating a space that is welcoming, safe, and warm will lead to learners maintaining the focus necessary to engage in an inquiry project from start to finish. Providing resources and instruction that enable learners to keep that focus then enables learners to be successful beyond the physical space of the school library and out into their learning community.

Questions for the Reflective Practitioner

1. What can I do to make learners' physical and virtual spaces more conducive to learning?

2. How can modeling self-reflection and focus when working with learners help them develop those dispositions?

3. How can I involve learners and educators more directly in developing a space that people want to be in for both personal and academic pursuits?

SHARE in Practice

chool librarians by nature are collaborative people willing to share knowledge and a love of literacy with other educators and learners in the community. Sharing is also one of the first things learners are taught when they start school. Social theorists such as Jean Piaget and Lev Vygotsky have stated that the best learning happens when there is collaboration and sharing. In planning for instruction, school librarians can use the strategies, tools, and example lessons included here. These examples are based on the Shared Foundation of Inquire and the Share Domain.

No-Tech Tools

When it comes to sharing new learning with others, learners should have voice and choice in determining how they present information. Depending on the type of inquiry unit of study, there are many ways for learners to present material to their learning community and beyond. When learners are ready to present products that demonstrate their learning, they can move beyond a poster presentation or a written response and consider models, 3-D diagrams, other visual art mediums, musical compositions, reproductions of artifacts, or museum exhibits. These variations support different learning styles and allow learners to demonstrate curiosity and initiative when showcasing their new learning. No-tech tools can also be used in reflection by the learner and as formative assessments by the school librarian and educator partner.

GALLERY WALKS

During inquiry, learners can put ideas they find interesting and want to explore into a Gallery Walk protocol. Gallery Walks engage learners as they move about the school library or classroom sharing ideas and responding to specific questions or ideas. Using sentence starters such as "I like . . . ," "I wonder . . . ," and "I have . . . ," learners can provide specific feedback to help each other move farther into the inquiry process. Learners can identify strengths in thinking and recognize gaps where more information or clarity is needed.

CIRCLE OF VIEWPOINTS

If learners are working in groups but need to address gaps, the Circle of Viewpoints protocol invites diverse perspectives. This routine helps learners consider diverse perspectives related to a topic. Understanding that people may think and feel differently about things is a key aspect of the Fairness Ideal, a module in Project Zero's Visible Thinking framework. Learners in groups explore each of the following discussion points by taking on a character and looking at the topic from different perspectives:

- I am thinking of [topic] from the point of view of [character].
- I think [describe the topic from your viewpoint].
- A question I have from this viewpoint is . . . .

COMPASS POINTS

The Compass Points routine is used to help learners evaluate their position. Learners brainstorm answers to questions based on the compass points E, W, N, and S:

E = Excited: What excites you about this idea or proposition? What's the upside?

W = Worrisome: What do you find worrisome about this idea or proposition? What's the downside?

N = Need to Know: What else do you need to know or find out about this idea or proposition? What additional information would help you to evaluate things?

S = Stance or Suggestion for Moving Forward: What is your current stance or opinion on the idea or proposition? How might you move forward in your evaluation of this idea or proposition? (Ritchhart et al., 2011, 93).

Low-Tech Tools

Depending on the availability of technology, there are many free programs that help learners decide how best to present their new knowledge. Microsoft, Apple, or Google writing tools can be used for presentations of learning. An alternative to writing an essay, blogging is a way for learners to demonstrate their learning to their learning community and beyond. If the school district uses a learning management system, there is a discussion board feature that learners can use to communicate online within the safety of the class environment. For older learners, using a blogging tool such as WordPress, Blogger, or Kidblog might be a way for learners to practice good digital citizenship while sharing their learning more globally.

Digital storytelling and podcasts are other ways for learners to showcase learning beyond an essay or poster display. There are digital publishing tools within Microsoft, Apple, and Google that can aid learners in producing video and audio products. If the district allows publishing beyond the classroom, the school library can have a YouTube channel that can showcase learning as well.

Microsoft, Apple, and Google have tools that allow learners to collaborate and give feedback as well as share their thinking with each other. Using word-processing software, learners can create outlines and storyboards and use other graphic organizers that allow other learners, the school librarian, and the classroom educator to provide feedback.

Using a learning management system, groups of learners working together can provide visible thinking during the inquiry process. School librarians and other educators can monitor learners as they progress through the project and provide real-time feedback.

 ## High-Tech Tools

High-tech tools can enhance the learning experience and create new opportunities for generating and sharing products with classmates, the school community, or a global audience. Learners, networked online, can more easily share information, work together on group projects, or present their work to the group. The following tools are curated from the AASL Best Websites for Teaching and Learning annual recognition program. Web tools previously mentioned that also have value in the Share Domain include Seesaw, Trello, Flipgrid, Book Creator, BoomWriter, and Kapwing.

MYSIMPLESHOW

The mysimpleshow online tool makes it easy to create narrated explanatory videos. Learners simply write a short script and choose images and animations, and mysimpleshow will do the rest. Voices are provided to do the narration, or learners can feel free to narrate the video themselves. Subtitles are available for better audience accessibility. This tool is appropriate for grades 4–12 when making videos and for grades K–12 when viewing videos.

SCREENCAST-O-MATIC

When you need to create how-to or flipped lesson (content that learners can view at their own pace or at home) videos for your school library or classroom, consider Screencast-O-Matic. It makes video editing and recording easy, and it is free for up to fifteen minutes of recording time. This is a great instructional tool for school librarians and other educators but is also appropriate for K–12 learners.

BUNCEE

Buncee is a presentation and digital storytelling tool great for creating interactive multimedia presentations. Learners, educators, and school librarians can integrate content using a wealth of sources as well as create within the program directly on each slide. Available via multiple platforms, Buncee is appropriate for grades K–12. This product has moved to a freemium status; the free version allows users to create three free presentations a month.

Example Lesson Plans for Share

The following lesson plans promote content-area collaboration and are aligned to Share Domain Competencies. These lessons feature the options of no-tech, low-tech, and high-tech tools and can be adapted to meet the needs of your learners, educator partners, and school library environment.

MANNERS MATTER

Grade Levels: K–2

Contributor: Lara Ivey

This lesson allows learners to be part of a process to establish routines and procedures in their school library. The lesson is adapted from the classbuilding idea included in the Kagan Cooperative Learning method (Kagan and Kagan 2015) to establish a safe, inviting, and accessible school library learning environment for all learners.

"I Can" Statement

I can help create and follow library procedures.

AASL Standards Framework for Learners

I.C.1. Learners adapt, communicate, and exchange learning products with others in a cycle that includes interacting with content presented by others.

Content Areas
History/Social Science

Duration
One 45-minute class session

Materials
- "Messy" school library area
- Chart paper, markers to record learners' thinking and suggestions
- Manners books from the Easy collection or short videos from YouTube

Lesson

Before: Learners will walk into the school library and find a mess. Ask learners what is wrong with what they see and record their answers.

During: Ask learners to read books curated about manners in school. After reviewing the books, ask learners why the mess in the school library is not acceptable and what suggestions they have about how to avoid messes in the future. Introduce the idea of procedures and ask learners to develop a list of procedures they think are important when entering, using, and exiting the school library. Post the list and allow each grade level to vote on the top five most important procedures that they agree to follow throughout the year.

Assessment: Assess learners on how well they follow their rules throughout the school year, especially after long breaks.

BECOMING AN AUTHOR

Grade Levels: K–2

Contributor: Lori Donovan

In this lesson, which takes place over several months, learners become authors and share their work with their peers. Working collaboratively with the art educator, learners can illustrate their books. The finished products can be put on display in the school library for others to read.

"I Can" Statement

I can write a children's book that I can share with my friends.

AASL Standards Framework for Learners

I.C.1. Learners adapt, communicate, and exchange learning products with others in a cycle that includes interacting with content presented by others.

I.C.2. Learners adapt, communicate, and exchange learning products with others in a cycle that includes providing constructive feedback.

I.C.3. Learners adapt, communicate, and exchange learning products with others in a cycle that includes acting on feedback to improve.

I.C.4. Learners adapt, communicate, and exchange learning products with others in a cycle that includes sharing products with an authentic audience.

Content Areas	Duration
Language Arts	Many 45-minute class sessions (this can be done
Mathematics	over the course of the school year where develop-
Computer Science	mentally appropriate)

Materials
- Various graphic organizers and storyboard templates
- Library catalog
- Book creation software such as Book Creator and BoomWriter (optional; this would shift the lesson from low-tech to high-tech)

Lesson

Before: Teach the elements of storytelling (beginning, middle, and end), plot, characters, and dialogue using a variety of genres and authors.

During: Ask learners to create their own stories using various graphic organizers and storyboarding templates and to participate in a reflection cycle that includes feedback from peers, the school librarian, and classroom educators. Learners will create and "publish" their books, which can be added to the school library catalog for checkout by peers (or posted in the online catalog if producing e-books).

Assessment: Assess learners throughout the process using online writing rubrics and peer feedback forms.

PET PERSUASION

Grade Levels: 3–5

Contributors: Heather Hess, Caroline Romano, Rita Saylor, Sue Strada, and Donald Walutes

This lesson is a continuation of the *Should a Tiger Be a Pet?* and *Just the Right Pet for Me!* lessons presented in parts II and III. This lesson continues the theme of finding the right pet for learners' families. Having learned that tigers are not good pets, learners researched different pets to see which pet would be a good fit for their family. Then they wrote persuasive letters to their parents asking for the pet they researched and explaining why that pet would be a good fit for their family. In this culminating lesson, learners use a presentation tool to report back to the class about whether their request was successful or not.

"I Can" Statement

I can use evidence to state my reasons for getting this pet.

AASL Standards Framework for Learners

I.C.2. Learners adapt, communicate, and exchange learning products with others in a cycle that includes providing constructive feedback.

I.C.4. Learners adapt, communicate, and exchange learning products with others in a cycle that includes sharing products with an authentic audience.

Content Areas
Language Arts
Science/STEM/STEAM

Duration
Two 45-minute class sessions

Materials

- PowerPoint, Sway (or other presentation tool)

Lesson

Before: Learners will reflect on how well their presentation of their persuasive letters to their parents went by answering the following questions:

- "What was your parents' reaction?"
- "Did you convince your parents?"
- "If you did not convince your parents, what steps will you take next?"
- "Whether or not you convinced them to get a pet, did you successfully convince your parents that the pet you selected is a great pet to own?"

During: Instruct learners in using an online presentation tool to create presentations giving advice to someone who wants to have the same pet that learners want or already have and explaining whether their persuasive letters were successful. Learners will create and share their presentations with their peers.

Assessment: Use peer and self-assessments, which can be found online, to help learners give and receive feedback on final products.

TOURING ANCIENT ROME

Grade Levels: 3–5

Contributor: Carolyn Moul

In this collaborative, three-day school library research project, learners will broaden their knowledge of ancient Rome by completing a ticket book of activities using a wide variety of learning centers in the school library. Other ancient civilizations can also be included following the same format.

"I Can" Statement
I can compare and contrast important elements about ancient civilizations.

AASL Standards Framework for Learners
I.C.1. Learners adapt, communicate, and exchange learning products with others in a cycle that includes interacting with content presented by others.

Content Areas
History/Social Science

Duration
Three 45-minute class sessions

Materials
- A variety of nonfiction books on ancient Rome
- Encyclopedias
- Atlases
- Online library catalog
- Britannica or another online database
- Discovery Education or another video streaming tool
- Google Earth
- Touring Ancient Rome passport (http://bit.ly/2JWcbuc) or a variety of questions that can be answered by your gathered resources

Lesson

Before: Teach mini-lessons on copyright and plagiarism. The classroom educator will instruct learners in nonfiction text features and note-taking.

During: During the first class period, learners will use a variety of books to answer questions in their passport about the ancient civilization of Rome. During the second class period, learners will use online databases and the school library catalog to further explore and to answer additional questions. During the third class period, learners will explore ancient Rome through tools like Google Earth and online videos. Learners will create a Works Cited list as they use sources to answer questions. For an extension lesson, ask learners to compare ancient Rome with ancient Greece according to the classroom educator's choice of vehicle (Venn diagram, poster, photo story project, etc.).

Assessment: Ask learners to reflect on their own research process and share new knowledge and ideas in a class discussion. Review learners' passports to assess understanding of copyright and fair use, assess works cited, and assess how well learners used nonfiction text features to answer research questions. The classroom educator will check content knowledge and application of skills when comparing ancient Rome with other ancient civilizations.

GET YOUR GAME ON!

Grade Levels: 6–8

Contributors: Laurie Bolt and Marie Taloute

In this lesson, learner groups are assigned an American colonial region to research and then develop a board game about with trivia questions and game play instructions. Then classmates will play the games, providing feedback on ease of play and new knowledge gained about the colony while playing the game. Groups will reflect on the feedback and make improvements to their product.

"I Can" Statements

I can provide feedback after playing a game created and shared by my peers.

I can use feedback from peers to make improvements to my game.

AASL Standards Framework for Learners

I.C.1. Learners adapt, communicate, and exchange learning products with others in a cycle that includes interacting with content presented by others.

I.C.2. Learners adapt, communicate, and exchange learning products with others in a cycle that includes providing constructive feedback.

I.C.3. Learners adapt, communicate, and exchange learning products with others in a cycle that includes acting on feedback to improve.

I.C.4. Learners adapt, communicate, and exchange learning products with others in a cycle that includes sharing products with an authentic audience.

Content Areas

History/Social Science

Duration

One 90-minute class session

Materials

- School library databases and nonfiction resources
- 3-D pens/printer
- Constructive Feedback form

Lesson

Before: Assign learner groups an American colonial region (South, Mid-Atlantic, or New England). Inform learners that they will be creating a board game representing the region assigned to their group. Provide instruction on locating information from print resources, formulating questions, and writing functional game play instructions. Learners will create questions (multiple choice, short answer, and true or false), game play instructions, and a game board and game pieces that reflect their region's resources, social and political life, specializations, and trivia.

During: Set up the completed, learner-created American colonies board games at tables in the school library before learners enter the space. Using a sample game board, the classroom educator begins with an overview of key game components (game pieces, question cards, and rules of play) and models how to complete the feedback form at each game table. Learners will then begin game play. When time is called, group members will complete the Constructive Feedback forms (created by the school librarian and educator partner) before moving on to the next game table. Learners should include a comment for each section on the form. Before game play resumes, learner groups will each read through the feedback received with their teammates. Groups will have a few minutes to reflect on positive remarks as well as suggested improvements and make any changes to their game during the time provided. Learners will have a second opportunity to play peer games and see how the feedback provided was incorporated by the creator group.

Assessment: Provide learners with a rubric or checklist of required elements to use in providing feedback to peers. Peer feedback may also include how easy the game was to play and how much new knowledge was gained about the colony while playing the game. Assess learners on how well they provided feedback to their peers. Alternatively or in addition, assess how well the learner groups used the feedback received to adjust their product, including closing gaps in learning product demonstration. An exit ticket can be used to prompt self-reflection from learners about the inquiry process, including what they would do differently in developing a future game and what went well or could be changed in the inquiry unit for future classes.

STUDY OF SONNETS

Grade Levels: 9–12

Contributor: Lori Donovan

In this lesson, learners experience different types of sonnets as part of their study of British literature. Then learners apply what they learn about sonnet style to their own creative writing. Learner-created sonnets can be posted on a class website or added to the school's literary magazine.

"I Can" Statement

I can research the different types of sonnet forms, analyze a popular sonnet of the form researched, write my own sonnet, and publish it to the class website.

AASL Standards Framework for Learners

I.C.4. Learners adapt, communicate, and exchange learning products with others in a cycle that includes sharing products with an authentic audience.

Content Area

Language Arts

Duration

Four 90-minute class sessions

Materials

- Critical analysis reference texts on sonnets
- Purdue Online Writing Lab (OWL) references for writing a research paper
- Academy of American Poets, Sonnet Central, and No Sweat Shakespeare have resources for educators, school librarians, and learners to use for writing sonnets
- Library databases

- NoodleTools
- Chromebooks
- Google Site

Lesson

Before: Learners will study three types of sonnets—Spenserian, Shakespearean, and Petrarchan/Italian—in class as part of their poetry unit, choosing a style to research and a sonnet to analyze.

During: In the school library, learners will research the selected sonnet form, find critical analyses of their sonnet to review, and write a research paper. Begin by conducting mini-lessons on using resources to provide analytical support and on paraphrasing and other note-taking strategies to aid learners while incorporating research into their commentary about their sonnet analysis. Learners will write their own sonnet in the format researched. Through a process of peer editing and classroom educator coaching, learners will publish their sonnets to a class website.

Assessment: Assess learners' information literacy skills such as narrowing a topic (the sonnet choice), navigating sources to analyze the sonnet, and citing sources correctly. The classroom educator will assess how well learners used research to support their analysis as well as other writing content skills assessments.

UNDERSTANDING GRAPHING USING STATISTICS

Grade Levels: 9–12

Contributor: Lori Donovan

Many algebra learners struggle with the concept of graphing. This collaborative lesson between the algebra instructor and the school librarian is an engaging way to help learners understand the elements of graphing.

"I Can" Statement

I can create a graph in a computer spreadsheet, correctly labeling x and y axes using information gathered from statistics on a topic of choice.

AASL Standards Framework for Learners

I.C.1. Learners adapt, communicate, and exchange learning products with others in a cycle that includes interacting with content presented by others.

Content Areas

Mathematics
STEM/STEAM

Duration

One 90-minute class session

Materials
- Excel or Google Sheets
- Lists of statistical sites for learners to choose
- Chart for copying data for insertion into graph or spreadsheet

Lesson

Before: Ask learners to choose a topic that has statistical data attached (sports, movie or song profits, favorite food, etc.).

During: Support learners as they research to find the data in graphic list format. Learners will use math skills in graphing to determine how to set up a line graph, a bar graph, data plot, and the like, and use an online spreadsheet application (Excel, Google Sheets) to plot information found during research. Once their graphs are complete, learners will share their graphs with their peers, explaining how they graphed their statistics using the academic language of graphing.

Assessment: Assess learners on their ability to read and use statistical data and turn that information into a graphic representation. Use of math concepts and graphing skills will be assessed by the classroom educator.

PART V

Grow

13

Growing Inquiry Learners

ny coach will tell players that practice increases the opportunity for success. Even in defeat there are lessons to be learned. The
focus is on how the player grows as an athlete and as a team member.
Malcolm Gladwell stated in his book *Outliers* that it takes ten thou-
sand hours of practice to become an expert in anything. Putting forth this effort is
how to grow. It is during these times of practice that learners grow themselves as
they apply new knowledge to prior knowledge.

The *National School Library Standards* state, "Learners grow each time they
iteratively question, create, share, and reflect on new knowledge; natural curiosity is sparked by means of this sustained inquiry cycle" (AASL 2018, 70). School
librarians and their educator partners work to develop learners' growth when they
collaborate to deliberately design inquiry units so that learners become efficient,
effective, and creative locators, accessors, and users of information. Through these
collaborative lessons, school librarians and their educator partners work together
to design experiences that will encourage learners to continually seek knowledge
through sustained inquiry that includes real-world applications and reflection to
guide informed decisions (AASL 2018, Learner I.D.1, I.D.2., I.D.3., I.D.4).

Continually Seeking and Engaging Knowledge

"Learners grow each time they iteratively question, create, share, and reflect on new
knowledge" through a sustained inquiry process (AASL 2018, 70). School librarians
and classroom educators work to develop inquiry-based projects that encourage
learners "to examine the authority of authors and the bias of sponsors; to assess

the importance of currency of information to the topic at hand; to determine the scope and relevance of information to meet their needs; and to create and share new ideas, resources, products, and information" (AASL 2019, 1).

The inquiry cycle needs to be planned carefully, with mini-lessons and scaffolds built in to sustain inquiry. These lessons can take place in the classroom as well as in the school library. Using questioning techniques described in previous chapters can aid in learner-developed questions that lead learners through a process to access, evaluate, and synthesize new knowledge to answer their research question or prove their hypothesis. Practicing question generation often in the school library and classroom settings prepares learners for the task of being curious and engaged to sustain inquiry throughout the learning unit.

Graphic organizers and inquiry logs or journals are scaffolds to help learners make connections as they examine resources for authority, accuracy, currency, and purpose. Lessons in evaluating sources for credibility and bias aid learners in developing critical-thinking skills that allow for understanding of diverse perspectives and viewpoints about their topic within an inquiry stance. These tools help learners continually seek knowledge as they answer questions and then develop more questions during the inquiry process.

Making Real-World Connections

Using learner-generated questions to sustain inquiry also connects learners to real-world applications. "When learners have support and scaffolds to be persistent and resilient during inquiry, they develop processes that enable them to make real-world connections" (AASL 2018, 70). Andrew Minigan, Sarah Westbrook, Dan Rothstein, and Luz Santana (2017) wrote that using the QFT can "deliberately teach students how to ask questions and [can] support students as they plan and drive their own inquiries, build their democratic thinking skills, become more information literate, and take informed civic action." Learner-generated questions naturally provide more engagement because learners have a hand in determining where the inquiry process is going. School librarians and classroom educators develop units so that they become guides for the learners as learners work through the learning unit.

As Wiggins and McTighe discussed in *Understanding by Design* (2005), educators and school librarians want to make sure that the lessons being developed are focused not only on specific content learning or a specific information literacy skill but also on a broader scope that can then be transferred to thinking beyond the unit. What connection can learners make that extends beyond this one learning experience? In GID, the learning team can bring new extensions or perspectives to the learning experience. Big6 wants learners to be able to take the skills of learning how to solve a problem or question and apply those skills to any other situation. The Stripling model and the Pathways to Knowledge protocol stress that school librarians and classroom educators need to drill down to what learners are most curious about and tap into that area. All these inquiry process models want educators and school librarians to build relationships with learners to help foster curiosity and initiative. If that can be done, engagement is there, and, as research shows, the best learning takes place.

Using Reflection to Guide Decisions

As learners become more adept at reviewing resources and determining purpose, reflection also needs to be a part of learning as they move through the inquiry process. When learners are first looking at possible resources, Stop and Jot sheets (graphic organizers used in the GID model) help them decide how to narrow resources to those that will best support them in answering their research questions or proving their hypotheses. Journaling and exit tickets are other ways that school librarians and their educator partners can determine where learners will need more resources or scaffolds during the inquiry process. "When learners have support and scaffolds to be persistent and resilient during inquiry, they develop processes that enable them to . . . reflect to guide informed decisions" (AASL 2018, 70).

School librarians and classroom educators need to model reflection for learners. Asking learners at the end of the unit to talk about what went well with the inquiry unit, what could be changed in the inquiry unit, and what advice they would give to the next set of learners who complete this unit encourages them to be reflective and shows that school librarians and classroom educators value their reflective voice as part of the inquiry process. School librarians and their educator partners include reflective assessments for learners throughout the inquiry unit. These intermittent assessments provide feedback for follow-up lessons during the unit and give learners an opportunity to build metacognitive skills—helping learners learn how they learn.

Questions for the Reflective Practitioner

1. Why is planning for sustained inquiry so important when designing an inquiry project?

2. How can I model persistence so that learners can continue within the inquiry process, even when hitting a stumbling block?

3. In what ways can I develop and sustain learners' persistence when they encounter challenges to their learning (roadblocks or failure)?

14

Empowering Learners to Grow

very good educator strives for all the learners in the class to be successful. Educators spend hours upon hours designing and delivering engaging learning opportunities that stretch learners' minds and challenge learners to move forward. School librarians are no different when they "implement and model an inquiry-based process" with learners (AASL 2018, School Librarian I.D.). AASL's position statement titled *Instructional Role of the School Librarian* affirms that the role of the school librarian is to guide learners and other educators through formal and informal learning activities using a range of information literacies and in both traditional and blended learning settings (AASL, forthcoming). Like the classroom educator, the school librarian works diligently to design and deliver engaging learning experiences to develop lifelong learners who want to seek knowledge, create new knowledge, and make real-world connections.

Leading and Modeling Inquiry Learning

Because the school library and school librarian serve the whole school population, it is important that the school librarian take an active role on the school's leadership team and the school's improvement plan. As part of the leadership team, the school librarian has an opportunity to participate in discussions about the school's goals and objectives. This position gives the school librarian information to guide provision of resources and learning opportunities for all to meet those school goals. If the school librarian is not part of the school's leadership team, it is imperative that the school librarian "[participate] in curriculum development and implementation through membership on instructional, curriculum, textbook, technology, professional development, and new program adoption committees" (AASL 2018, 174). Using the information gathered from these committees, school librarians can seek out professional journal articles and social media posts to help provide researched-based resources and ideas to meet the school's development goals.

Once the school librarian has obtained the information needed to help meet the school's goals, then the librarian needs to develop a plan for how the school library can best serve its stakeholders. "The school librarian collaborates with educators to design and teach engaging inquiry-based learning experiences as well as assessments that incorporate multiple literacies and foster critical thinking" (AASL 2018, 174). Each of the inquiry-based research methods walks educators and learners through this process. Think about which inquiry process model would work best in your school's community and work to implement it.

Why is an inquiry-learning stance this important when "leading learners and staff through the research process" (AASL 2018, School Librarian I.D.1.)? Because it engages learners with content to build on prior knowledge, enable real-world practice of critical and creative thinking, and highlight communication and collaboration skills. Providing professional development to educator partners on inquiry-based learning highlights the instructional partner role as well as presenting the school librarian as an information specialist. "Work smarter, not harder" is a mantra that the school librarian can demonstrate by promoting collaboration models that learners can see when learners themselves are working collaboratively with their peers.

Each of the inquiry process models previously described breaks down the inquiry process into steps that allow the school librarian and educator partner to hone skills that learners need at each stage of the process. These inquiry models also provide opportunities at each stage for self-reflection by learners on process and product. If school librarians and their educator partners can see where academic reading and writing can be incorporated through an inquiry process that engages learners' curiosity and initiative, the knowledge gained and retained increases exponentially. The inquiry process also builds learners' abilities to transfer those skills into new inquiry learning units within and outside core content levels.

Constructing Focused Tasks

One of the main tenets of inquiry-based learning is that it is learner-centric. "The school librarian empowers learners to create new knowledge in an inquiry-based research process aligned to each learner's interests" (AASL 2018, 72). Inquiry-based learning begins by posing questions or problems that need to be answered or solved rather than focusing on the distribution of facts. "Constructing tasks focused on learners' individual areas of interest" allows learners to connect prior knowledge to new knowledge by making connections to the world in which they live (AASL 2018, School Librarian I.D.2).

Research from Indiana University Bloomington revealed that all inquiry-based learning has these five general elements in common (Heick 2017):

- Learning focuses on a meaningful, well-structured problem that demands consideration of diverse perspectives.
- Academic content-learning occurs as a natural part of the process as learners work toward finding solutions.
- Learners, working collaboratively, assume an active role in the learning process.
- Educators provide learners with learning supports and rich multiple media sources of information to assist learners in successfully finding solutions.
- Learners share and defend solutions publicly in some manner.

Heick (2017) then described the four phases of inquiry. School librarians and other educators become the "meddler in the middle" during the inquiry process.

- *Interaction:* Learners "dive into engaging, relevant, and credible media forms to identify a 'need' or opportunity for inquiry. . . . Tone [is] open-minded, curious, unburdened, playful" [Discovery in Appreciative Inquiry].
- *Clarification:* Learners summarize and categorize data and understanding with classroom educator or expert support. Tone is slightly more focused, reflective, and independent [Dream in Appreciative Inquiry].
- *Questioning:* Learners ask relevant questions to drive continued, self-directed inquiry. Tone is discerning, confident, interdependent, and productive [Destiny in Appreciative Inquiry].
- *Design:* Learners design an accessible, relevant, and curiosity-driven action or product to justify inquiry. Tone is creative, efficient, calculating, and enthusiastic [Design in Appreciative Inquiry].

All the inquiry process models reflect each of these stages within an inquiry unit. Teaching learners these processes builds learners' metacognitive skills to become independent lifelong users and creators of information. Practicing these skills allows learners to "[enact] new understanding through real-world connections" (AASL 2018, Learner I.D.3.).

Seeking, Creating, Connecting New Knowledge

Instructional planning and delivery must be purposeful in intent—learners need to gain knowledge in content areas that apply prior knowledge to new knowledge in an engaging format that is transferable to other learning within that content-area subject. For school librarians this means that information literacy skills and the appropriate use of educational technology are integrated with core content materials. The school librarian fosters a "growth mindset [that] enables all learners to seek knowledge, create new meaning, and make real-world connections for lifelong learning"

(AASL 2018, 72). Berger (2016) and others have reminded educators that learners must be prepared to apply critical and creative thinking in contexts that haven't been developed yet. Therefore, these writers have argued that the skills needed by learners to succeed are the abilities to inquire, think critically, and problem solve.

Real-world learning allows learners to see and understand why what they are learning is useful beyond school. How many educators and school librarians have been asked by learners, "Why do we have to do this?" "Because I said so!" is not an answer. Education in the twentieth century was focused on industrial age thinking—that schools were preparing learners to be good citizens and effective factory workers. Those who were able to grasp concepts quickly and easily moved into management. Learners who were lucky enough to go to college got to be in the boardroom. However, in today's global economy, that is not how education should work to guarantee learners' success when they leave the K–12 environment. The purpose of education in the twenty-first century is to prepare learners for life—especially for life with technology.

As school librarians and educator partners collaboratively plan inquiry projects, the first major connection to the real world should stem from the learner's curiosity: "How does learning this impact my life and the lives of those around me?" Using Appreciative Inquiry to dream what is possible provides a framework for learners to see the relevance of their learning to themselves and others. By working collaboratively and developing communication skills, learners see connections to problems and are able to create hypotheses, solutions, and answers through their new knowledge.

School librarians can work with educator partners to incorporate real-world experiences into lessons by curating resources to help learners through the inquiry process. These resources include not only the print and digital items typically found in a school library but also local historical groups and museums that maintain primary sources, or guest speakers who are experts in the field that learners are exploring in an inquiry process. Current events and news can be connected to the inquiry process and teach learners important media literacy lessons as well. In addition, learners need to curate and express their learning in meaningful ways beyond the traditional written or oral report. How can learners express their learning to a more-global audience? What technology tools can be incorporated into the curation of new knowledge and serve as models for the tools used by people in the field of study?

Creating as part of the inquiry process allows learners much voice and choice in how they present their new learning. Connecting learners with experts (either in person or by Skype) and with resources found in the school library helps learners showcase the products of their inquiry and apply new knowledge to the content area being studied. Creating products that illustrate learning is just as important as the inquiry learning process itself.

Questions for the Reflective Practitioner

1 How can learners use their new knowledge to create a demonstration of their learning for others?

2 Why should I work to make real-world connections to learning, even for the youngest of learners?

3 How can creating learning experiences enhance the school's culture of inquiry?

15

Growing an Inquiry Culture in the School Library

ere's a warning from George Couros: "If students leave school less curious than when they started, we have failed them" (Couros 2015, 6). How do school librarians and their educator partners work to keep learners engaged and curious during their time in the school library and classroom to meet the challenge expressed by Couros? What does that inquiry culture look like? How do school librarians and their educator partners move learners from compliance to engagement to empowerment? How do school librarians and their educator partners establish and support a learning environment that builds critical-thinking and inquiry dispositions which capture the learners' sparks of curiosity and then let that curiosity lead learners through the inquiry process?

To answer those questions, look at the school library itself. What is it about the space that makes learners come into it? What is the school librarian doing to create a supportive learning environment that makes learners want to come in and see more? What is the school librarian doing beyond instruction that will encourage those who are reluctant to come in? Shel Silverstein's poem "Invitation" asks a variety of people to come in. What invitation has the school librarian sent out? How can the school library be a curiosity factory? School librarians "[reinforce] the role of the school library, information, and technology resources in maximizing learning and institutional effectiveness" (AASL 2018, School Library I.D.2.). Thinking about the learning culture in the school community can help guide the school librarian to develop an inquiry plan that supports learners and moves them forward to that culture of inquiry.

Establishing and Supporting Learning Environments

Current trends in ways to encourage creativity and curiosity, such as makerspaces and design and computational thinking, can be used in inquiry projects as well as in learning stations that are open during school hours. How can a gaming philosophy be used in the school library to promote creative- and critical-thinking skills? "In an effective school library, school librarians innovate, implement, and model an inquiry-based process for learners. So that learners and other educators in the school see the inquiry process presented in authentic ways, inquiry demonstrations may occur in a faculty meeting, in a nontraditional classroom, or with a small subgroup of learners" (AASL 2018, 73).

In what ways is the school librarian promoting inquiry learning through modeling and instruction to help foster the inquiry culture within your school? Normal school structures do not really allow for the collaboration needed to truly develop an inquiry culture. "The schools must create structures that support flexible learning teams that have time to design, implement, and reflect together. . . . Priorities need to change from compliant behaviors to an innovative professional culture where the priority is learning that helps [learners] engage in the world of today. The priority in inquiry schools depends on collaboration, flexible organization, and information literacy" (Kuhlthau et al., 2015, 175).

Inquiry learning and the inquiry process models require professional development for administrators and educator partners. The school library works in collaboration to establish and support a learning environment that assists learners to achieve and "that builds critical-thinking and inquiry dispositions for all learners" (AASL 2018, School Library I.D.1.). If the school community is beginning its journey to develop a culture of inquiry, think about small, incremental steps. Working with a subject area or grade level can be a way to begin to integrate this inquiry culture. Grab the new educators in the building during work week and talk to them about how the school library can support their curriculum—and to paraphrase *Field of Dreams,* "If you feed them, they will come!"

Integrating School Library Instruction with Core Content

To get learners into the school library curiosity lab, it must have resources that inspire curiosity. A quality collection will contain robust selections that support academic and personal pursuits. The physical space will lend itself to multiple grouping formats depending on needs, as described in previous chapters. Having a variety of resources on topics and multiple viewpoints helps build learners' capacity for inquiry and critical and creative thinking. Collaborating with educators in developing these inquiry projects shows that "systematic and deliberate inquiry builds critical-thinking dispositions throughout the school learning community" (AASL 2018, 73).

The school librarian as information specialist should be the go-to person in the building for information needs. Communicating with educator partners about resources and tools to help with learning and teaching is a simple way to let others know that the school library is the place to look for things they didn't even know they were looking for. As an educator, teaching other educators and learners how to navigate and use information ethically and responsibly demonstrates that there is a trusted source for using information within a global society.

"As part of the school library, the school librarian provides leadership and instruction to both educators and learners on how to use all of [the] resources constructively, ethically, and safely" (AASL 2019, 1). The school librarian offers expertise in accessing and evaluating information and collections of quality physical and virtual resources. In addition, the school librarian possesses dispositions that encourage broad and deep exploration of ideas and responsible use of information technologies. These attributes add value to the school community.

"A real-world connection means that students see a reason to do this project, other than the fact that [an educator] assigned it and they will get a grade on it" (Simkins et al., 2002). The best way to engage learners is to explain why they are learning the content and how it relates to their lives. This is why the planning team is so important. Yes, there is much work up front on the part of the school librarian and educator partner, but if the goal is transferable knowledge, then engagement is key. Making connections to real-world applications is one way to secure this engagement.

This approach doesn't mean that learners need to leave the school in order to connect to the real world. Technology allows learners to have experts at their fingertips. Using online databases and web searches, learners can tap into information that leads to connecting learning to life. Skype and Google Hangouts bring experts to the learners without their leaving the school grounds. If your district lets learners have e-mail accounts, e-mailing experts or doing an online questionnaire can give learners necessary information to complete an inquiry project.

In the book *Increasing Student Learning through Multimedia Projects,* the authors offer ten ways to make connections in three different categories:

- Connecting through Project Topics
    - » Connecting through [learner] interests
    - » Connecting through [learner] experiences
    - » Connecting through significant issues

- Connecting through Interaction
    - » Improving the real world
    - » Relating to clients
    - » Interacting with assessors
    - » Interacting with people who know

- Connecting to the Future
  - » Learning adult work and life skills
  - » Creating a body of work
  - » Creating images of the future (Simkins et al., 2002)

Using these categories as a starting point and seeing what content area makes them possible, school librarians and other educators can develop an inquiry project that engages learners not only with the content but also with making those connections to learning beyond the classroom and into possible careers.

"Continuous modeling and implementation reinforces the role of the school library and its resources in maximizing learning, creating new knowledge and institutional effectiveness" (AASL 2018, 73). This modeling can include lessons on how to know which resource or expert to consult and lessons on how to look for prejudice or bias when dealing with a controversial topic. Modeling how to break down information into smaller bites will help learners gain insight into developing the disposition to continue even when encountering a roadblock. Lessons that model ethical information use and media production are ways to showcase information literacy while the educator partner moves the content learning forward.

Working to grow learners into productive citizens is a job that all educator partners and stakeholders must embrace. Using an inquiry process model is one of the best ways to design learning that reinforces growth opportunities, and there is no better place to be part of that learning than in the school library.

Questions for the Reflective Practitioner

1. How can learners grow in their inquiry learning to make content and real-world connections?

2. How can I work with other educators to ensure that learners have an opportunity to grow in their personal and academic pursuits and make real-world connections?

3. How can the culture of inquiry in a school teach learners how to question better to add to content knowledge and build the disposition to learn from failure and keep moving forward?

GROW in Practice

very day, school librarians shape student learners into pro-ductive, lifelong learners. The goal is to grow learners into adults who engage in sustained inquiry, continually seek out new knowledge to grow themselves, reflect on their learning to inform their decision making, and use that learning to affect the communities where they live in positive ways. The strategies, tools, and example lessons included here are based on using the Shared Foundation of Inquire in the research process, reflecting the dispositions learners develop through the Grow Domain.

No-Tech Tools

Applying learning to real-world situations engages learners with the opportunity to see how learning extends beyond the classroom. No-tech tools can be used to create real-world experiences through simulations and presentations of information learned. For example, written and phone interviews with experts are no-tech tools that learners can use to simulate real-world applications.

No-tech tools that help learners reflect as they work through the inquiry process include exit tickets, checklists, rating scales of work progress, inquiry journals, and matrixes. A great resource for developing and using no-tech tools for reflection is Violet Harada and Joan Yoshina's book, *Assessing for Learning: Librarians and Teachers as Partners* (2010).

WHAT MAKES YOU SAY THAT?

What Makes You Say That? is a thinking routine that asks learners to describe something, such as an object or a concept, and then support their interpretation with evidence. The routine promotes evidential reasoning (evidence-based reasoning), and because it invites learners to share their interpretations, it encourages them to understand alternatives and multiple perspectives. Good question starters for the group include "What is going on?" or "What do you see to make you say that?" or "What evidence do you have to support that statement?" This routine encourages critical and creative thinking as well as the communication skills that learners need in order to support a claim using evidence (Ritchhart et al., 2011, 165).

SENTENCE-PHRASE-WORD

Sentence-Phrase-Word is a text-rendering protocol that helps learners identify strengths and gaps in their research during the inquiry process. Learners will review the text that they have read and select a *sentence* that was meaningful to them and helped them gain a deeper understanding of the text; a *phrase* that moved, engaged, provoked, or was meaningful to them; and a *word* that captured their attention or struck them as powerful. It is useful to have learners write their sentence, phrase, and word on three separate sticky notes. Learners then share their findings with the group. The group will look for patterns that individual learners can use to move forward with their inquiry (Ritchhart et al., 2011, 207).

I USED TO THINK . . . , BUT NOW I THINK . . .

The I Used to Think . . . , But Now I Think . . . protocol is a great reflection tool that helps learners connect prior and background knowledge to new learning and be reflective in the process. The protocol can be useful in consolidating new learning as learners identify their new understandings, opinions, and beliefs. By examining and explaining how and why their thinking has changed, learners are developing their reasoning abilities and recognizing cause-and-effect relationships (Ritchhart et al., 2011, 154).

THE EXPLANATION GAME

The Explanation Game is a good fit for understanding why something is the way it is. This routine can get at causal explanation or explanation in terms of purpose or both. The routine focuses first on identifying something interesting about an object or idea—"I notice that . . ."—and then follows with the question, "Why is it that way?" or "Why did it happen that way?" The group works together to build explanations rather than deferring to an outside source, such as the educator or a textbook, to provide an answer (Ritchhart et al., 2011, 101).

Low-Tech Tools

Low-tech tools are good for learners who have access to a lab or a class set of computers to aid in their inquiry process. Whatever technology the district has—Microsoft, Google, Apple—there are template tools within their platforms that allow learners to work through an inquiry process. In the planning stages, the school librarian and educator partner need to determine which template tool is best for the job at hand. ReadWriteThink templates aid learners' inquiry journey. Google Draw has templates for creating a visual representation of learners' inquiry in lots of subject areas.

Similar online tools that learners can access easily include Padlet, an online bulletin board; Lino, an online web sticky note tool; and Scrible Edu, a freemium online tool that aids in researching because it allows learners to annotate, helps them create citations, and integrates with Google Drive.

Learners can use the low-tech presentation tools within Microsoft, Google, and Apple platforms. Within these platforms, there are also collaboration tools that foster group work. Microsoft tools that allow for collaboration include OneDrive, Outlook, Office 365 Groups, Microsoft Teams, and Delve boards. Google collaboration tools include Gmail; Google Calendar; and Google Docs, Sheets, Keep, Slides, and Hangouts. Apple tools include Slack, Join.Me, Buffer, Hive Learning, Basecamp, and If This Then That (IFTTT). Interviews with experts in the field using Skype and Google Hangouts are an easy way to connect learners with people in a timely manner, no matter where the learners or the experts are.

Some low-tech tools help learners with reflection or allow for real-time assessment and immediate feedback from school librarians and other educators. Using digital recorders or online sites such as VoiceThread allows learners to record their thoughts as they work, and the MP3/4 files can be shared with the school librarian and classroom educator.

High-Tech Tools

High-tech tools can drive learner growth by helping learners understand where they are and where they are going. Allowing learners voice and choice in selecting the high-tech tools they will use to present their learning product provides learners an opportunity to work in a real-world simulation of the information presentations that many careers or employers ask of their workers. These tools come from AASL's Best Websites for Teaching and Learning. Other tools that have been mentioned before—Glogster, Prezi, BoomWriter, Flipgrid, and YouTube—are also used in real-world simulations of working with and presenting newly gained information.

RECAP

Recap facilitates deeper, more-empowering online discussions by combining the options of chat and video for learner responses. The site involves participants in a moderated, question-led dialogue using chat to get conversations started and video to explore thoughts more deeply. Learners may be invited to answer questions in a queue, encouraged to dig deeper into a topic through a journey (a collection of prompts), or asked to add their own questions. Sharing may be with the educator, with the class, or with the world.

STANFORD HISTORY EDUCATION GROUP

Stanford History Education Group provides history lessons and assessments that teach learners to use primary sources and explore historical inquiry. Free online lessons help educator partners of older learners cover topics such as digital literacy, civic reasoning, and information literacy skills. Numerous assessments of various information literacy skills are provided. The assessments can be used to determine learners' existing knowledge, to design relevant information literacy lessons, and to spark discussions about digital content.

PIXICLIP

PixiClip, an online whiteboard, allows learners to create a video to demonstrate their learning. It is especially engaging for learners with an interest in graphic arts.

EXPLAIN EVERYTHING

The Explain Everything app is an online whiteboard that allows learners to incorporate multiple formats of texts, pictures, videos, and the like. For older learners doing extensive multimedia projects, Explain Everything is a handy tool for organizing many different formats of media into one cohesive piece to share.

KAIZENA

Kaizena offers users the ability to embed voice comments, text comments, and links to learners' work. Educators or peers highlight the text they want to comment on and then click to embed comments or links. Kaizena is a great resource for older learners (grades 6–12), giving feedback in a variety of formats. Kaizena syncs with Google Drive for easy access to documents in that format, but users can sign up without Google Drive as well.

Example Lesson Plans for Grow

The following lesson plans promote content-area collaboration and are aligned to Grow Domain Competencies. These lessons feature the options of no-tech, low-tech, and high-tech tools and can be adapted to meet the needs of your learners, educator partners, and school library environment.

STATES OF MATTER

Grade Levels: K–2

Contributor: Lori Donovan

This lesson encourages younger learners to think like a scientist in the school library. Using stations, learners will observe the school librarian using simple objects to conduct experiments that show the states of matter. Learners will write about or draw what they see in their scientific notebook, and they will journal about what happens when a solid becomes a liquid and then a gas.

"I Can" Statement

I can state the differences between a solid, a liquid, and a gas.

AASL Standards Framework for Learners

I.D.2. Learners participate in an ongoing inquiry-based process by engaging in sustained inquiry.

Content Area

Science

Duration

One 45-minute class session

Materials

- *What Is the World Made Of? All About Solids, Liquids, and Gases* by Kathleen Weidner Zoehfeld (or any other book about states of matter)
- Chart paper, markers to record learners' hypotheses
- Science journal

Lesson

Before: Set up a lab station to turn ice to water to a gas. Ask learners what scientists do when they experiment. (Answer: Scientists make a hypothesis, or guess, about what they think will happen.) Ask learners what they think happens to ice when it is left out of the freezer. Write their answers on chart paper.

During: Read *What Is the World Made Of? All About Solids, Liquids, and Gases* by Kathleen Weidner Zoehfeld. Give each learner a science journal. Ask learners to observe what happens to ice when it is heated, moving from a solid to a liquid to a gas, and to record their observations in their journal. Ask learners to share what they saw and compare that observation to their hypotheses or guesses that were noted on the chart paper. Learners should be able to say that increasing the temperature was the reason the ice became a liquid and then a gas. (If doing this activity with second graders, the school librarian can add academic vocabulary such as *evaporation* and *water cycle* to the lesson.)

Assessment: Assess learners on how well they can demonstrate the differences between a solid, a liquid, and a gas, or on how well they communicated their observations to each other. Share these assessments with your educator partner.

FALL PUMPKIN RESEARCH

Grade Levels: K–2

Contributor: Carolyn Vibbert

This lesson, built around a trip to a pumpkin farm, gives K–2 learners experience asking questions, finding answers, and showing that what they know makes sense. This four-week unit introduces learners to the ideas of Inquire and gives them an opportunity to share their learning with an authentic audience.

"I Can" Statements

I can ask questions to help me learn new things.
I can read to find the answers to my questions.
I can show what I learned with pictures.

AASL Standards Framework for Learners

I.D.2. Learners participate in an ongoing inquiry-based process by engaging in sustained inquiry.
I.D.3. Learners participate in an ongoing inquiry-based process by enacting new understanding through real-world connections.

Content Area

Science

Duration

Four 45-minute class sessions

Materials

- Sentence strips
- Markers in several colors
- PebbleGo (or other age-appropriate library database)
- Books about fall and pumpkins
- Bulletin board paper
- Construction paper and found objects from outside and recycling
- Glue, scissors, pencils, crayons, and the like

Lesson Day 1: Questioning

Before: Preceding a trip to the pumpkin farm, set the scene by telling learners that authors must learn new things before they are an expert and that when learners ask questions and learn new things, they are doing research.

During: Ask learners what they know about pumpkins. Use one color marker for writing what learners think they know about fall and pumpkins. Record a variety of statements from learners, even if they are factually inaccurate. Emphasize that these statements are things we *think* we know. Support learners by drawing little pictures along with text. Re-read all the statements with learners.

Transition to questioning. Ask learners what questions they have about pumpkins. Switch marker colors. If needed, use preselected pictures of fall or pumpkins to spark ideas for questions. Kindergarten learners need practice phrasing questions. Use sentence stems to lead into questions and help learners rephrase statements into questions. Encourage a variety of questions. Restate questions that have already been asked, as needed. Draw picture cues to help learners identify the words used in the writing. Re-read all the questions. Reemphasize that learners and authors ask questions to help them learn new information. Together, the class will read to learn the answers to the questions during the next class session.

Lesson Day 2: Using PebbleGo

Remind learners that they are being researchers to learn about fall and pumpkins. Explain that during the previous class session, we wrote down what learners know about fall and pumpkins. [Read the statements.] Remind learners that they wanted to learn new information, so they asked questions to help them learn. [Read the questions.] Explain that today learners will be answering some of the questions they asked during the previous session.

Show learners how to access and use PebbleGo from home. Locate, read, and discuss the article that will help answwer one question the best. Ask learners to dictate what the new sentence should say (use a third color). Repeat the exercise with a second question. Wrap up with a review of what learners know, the questions they answered today, and the questions that remain.

Lesson Day 3: Learning from Books

Use nonfiction texts related to the questions and repeat the process from day 2. Wrap up with reviewing everything learners have learned. Inform learners that authors show what they learned by writing books, but learners will show what they learned by creating a mural.

Lesson Day 4: Mural Creation

Assemble mural supplies and assign learner groups a sentence strip with a fact (not a question). Explain that learner groups will draw or create a picture showing what they know or learned. Learners can create by cutting and gluing paper, drawing, or using collected items. When items are ready, place them on the mural into a scene along with the sentence strips (information and questions) used throughout the research process. Glue all the elements down and hang the mural in the hallway.

Assessment: Debrief with learners by reading the mural together. Emphasize starting with questions and ending with showing what learners learned.

A PET FOR MY PEERS

Grade Levels: 3–5

Contributors: Heather Hess, Caroline Romano, Rita Saylor, Sue Strada, and Donald Walutes

This lesson is the culmination of the lessons about pets presented in parts II, III, and IV. This lesson continues the theme of finding the right pet for learners' families. At the end of the lesson, learners will practice giving feedback to help their peers choose the right pet. Learners will take the feedback from their peers and further reflect on what they have learned.

"I Can" Statements

I can reflect on my learning about choosing the right pet.

I can give and receive feedback about my work and others' work.

AASL Standards Framework for Learners

I.D.3. Learners participate in an ongoing inquiry-based process by enacting new understanding through real-world connections.

I.D.4. Learners participate in an ongoing inquiry-based process by using reflection to guide informed decisions.

Content Areas

Language Arts

Science/STEM/STEAM

Duration

One 45-minute class session

Materials

- Presentation slides
- Feedback form
- Reflection questionnaire
- Reflection journal

Lesson

Before: Instruct learners on how to give specific, helpful, and kind feedback to each other.

During: After learners share their presentations from the previous lesson with class-mates, ask learners to complete feedback forms and return them to their peers. Give learners an opportunity to reflect on the feedback they received from their peers, then ask learners to independently consider and respond to the following questions:

- "Based on what you have learned, would you still choose the same pet? Explain."
- "How did your audience react to your request?"
- "What conditions did your audience place on getting this pet?"
- "Are these conditions fair?"

- "Do you need to find out more information before you are able to get this pet?"
- "After gathering all this information, would you still want the pet? Is owning a pet worth the cost and responsibility?"

Next, lead a class discussion about the various places that animals call home (shelters, zoos, sanctuaries). Ask learners, "Why do animals live in shelters, zoos, and sanctuaries?" "What purposes do zoos serve?" "How does this knowledge about shelters, zoos, and sanctuaries relate to how you think about pet ownership?"

Finally, ask learners to reflect on what they have learned by responding to the following writing prompt in their reflection journals: "Based on the activities you have completed, discuss what you have learned about animals and pet care. Be sure to explain how you feel about responsible pet care and society's perception of pet ownership. Then discuss humanity's global responsibility to wildlife."

Assessment: Assess writing skills in each learner's reflection journal. Also, assess each learner's "explanation" to a new friend. These two outputs are useful measures of how well learners understood the process of research and inquiry.

FOLKTALE AND FAIRY TALE COMPARISON

Grade Levels: 3–5

Contributor: Carolyn Moul

In this unit, learners, working in groups, use a Venn diagram to compare and contrast the good and bad qualities of folktale or fairy-tale characters. Learners learn the elements of folktales, analyze characters, and highlight similarities and dissimilarities of the items being compared in graphic form.

"I Can" Statement

I can compare and contrast elements of folktale and fairy-tale styles.

AASL Standards Framework for Learners

I.D.2. Learners participate in an ongoing inquiry-based process by engaging in sustained inquiry.

Content Areas

English/Language Arts

Duration

Three 90-minute class sessions
or six 30-minute class sessions

Materials

- *Borreguita and the Coyote: A Tale from Ayutla, Mexico* by Verna Aardema, illustrated by Petra Mathers
- A variety of other folktales and fairy tales (Red Riding Hood, Cinderella, etc.)
- Crayons
- Poster paper

Lesson

Before: Before learners come to the school library, the classroom educator will read aloud *Borreguita and the Coyote* and discuss the elements of a folktale. Once at the library, learners will choose a partner and pick out a new folktale or fairy tale to read.

During: Each pair of learners will discuss the characters in their selected folktale or fairy tale and create a Venn diagram comparing the good characters to Borreguita and the bad characters to the coyote. Each pair of partners will also create a poster to represent the characteristics of a good or bad character. The partners then will present their Venn diagram and poster to the class.

Assessment: Assess learners on how well they were able to represent their fairy tale or folktale in the final product. In addition, assess their verbal presentation to their peers.

FAKE NEWS GALLERY WALK

Grade Levels: 6–8

Contributors: Patty Lambusta and Laurie Bolt

This is a culminating lesson of an inquiry unit on learning about fake news and how to use critical-thinking skills to spot it. Applying skills taught through the inquiry process, learners researched a topic of their choice and, using the CRAAP test, identified one credible source, one mediocre source, and one unreliable source. CRAAP is an acronym for Currency, Relevance, Authority, Accuracy, and Purpose. By employing the CRAAP test while evaluating sources, learners reduce the likelihood of using unreliable information. Learners then wrote a justification for labeling each of their source selections as reliable, mediocre, or unreliable. In this lesson, learners will display those justifications and a mock-up of their final project to be peer reviewed in a Gallery Walk protocol. Finally, using a format of their choice (nondigital or digital), learners will create a project (e.g., storyboard, trifold, website, digital presentation, etc.) to present their research findings.

"I Can" Statements

I can share new knowledge regarding fake news with my peers.

I can use constructive feedback to reflect on new knowledge.

AASL Standards Framework for Learners

I.D.3. Learners participate in an ongoing inquiry-based process by enacting new understanding through real-world connections.

I.D.4. Learners participate in an ongoing inquiry-based process by using reflection to guide informed decisions.

Content Areas

English/Language Arts

Duration

One 90-minute class session

Materials

- Various presentation programs (optional)
- *Austin's Butterfly: Building Excellence in Student Work* (video; https://modelsofexcellence.eleducation.org/resources/austins-butterfly)
- Opinion stem posters
- Sticky notes

Lesson

Before: Learners set up their fake news mock-up projects in the library in preparation for the Gallery Walk. Show learners the six-minute video, *Austin's Butterfly,* to encourage the feedback process and set norms on how to participate in a Gallery Walk. Prepare suggested opinion stems—for example, "I like . . . because . . . ," "I wonder . . . ," and "I have a suggestion, an idea, a resource . . . ."

During: Ask learners to review peer projects via a Gallery Walk. Provide sticky notes and opinion stem posters at each project station. Require learners to evaluate three to five projects, leaving feedback for each project.

Following the Gallery Walk, learners will return to their project station and read peer feedback. Using that feedback, learners will write a statement about how this project experience will impact future selection of resources. Learners will include a statement about the process (Gallery Walk) and the impact of sharing new knowledge within their learning community.

Assessment: Assess learners on how well they were able to determine and present authentic information about their topic for the feedback session and how well they provided feedback. Using Ron Berger's *Austin's Butterfly* as a model, assess whether learners provided feedback that was specific, helpful, and kind. Last, assess how learners used the feedback to improve their product to demonstrate their new learning.

EXPLORING SOCIAL JUSTICE THEMES IN *TO KILL A MOCKINGBIRD*

Contributors: Shelley Armstrong and Daniel McCulley

With the help of an inquiry log, learners make connections between a classic novel from 1960 and a social justice issue currently impacting the world. Learners will present their new connections in a research paper.

"I Can" Statement

I can connect events in the novel to social justice themes today.

AASL Standards Framework for Learners

I.D.1. Learners participate in an ongoing inquiry-based process by continually seeking knowledge.

I.D.3. Learners participate in an ongoing inquiry-based process by enacting new understanding through real-world connections.

Content Areas

Language Arts
History/Social Science

Duration

Four 90-minute class sessions

Materials

- Google Classroom
- Chromebooks
- Library databases
- *To Kill a Mockingbird* by Harper Lee

Lesson

Before: Have learners read *To Kill a Mockingbird* and research the social injustice themes and issues in the novel. Ask, "How do events and figures of the civil rights movement, roles of women in the 1930s, and the Great Depression relate to the social injustices in Harper Lee's *To Kill a Mockingbird* and in our country today?"

During: Before learners come to the school library, the classroom educator will ask learners to brainstorm current events that they feel reflect the issues raised in Lee's book and then narrow the list to a topic of interest to research. The school librarian will support learners as they research the social justice issue and, using their inquiry logs, make connections between the novel and the present-day social justice issue in preparation for writing a research paper.

Assessment: Assess learners on time management, digital citizenship, peer editing of their research paper rough drafts, and conferences with the classroom educator and school librarian.

HAS "THE DREAM" BECOME REALITY?

Grade Levels: 9–12

Contributors: Heather Murfee and Emily Mazzanti

This multimedia lesson utilizes Google Maps to deliver U.S. history content and Google Docs to facilitate both independent and peer-to-peer learning. Learners collaboratively build new knowledge as they explore resources pertaining to the key people and events of the civil rights era and other movements in the fight for equality.

"I Can" Statements

I can identify the measures used during the civil rights era by the three branches of the federal government and explain the relationship between causes and effects and their impact on promoting greater racial equality.

I can use specific and relative evidence about civil rights events to explain how relative context influenced historical development.

I can analyze relationships among different regional, social, ethnic, and racial groups and explain how these groups' experiences have changed over time.

AASL Standards Framework for Learners

I.D.1. Learners participate in an ongoing inquiry-based process by continually seeking knowledge.

Content Areas

History/Social Science

Duration

Two 90-minute class sessions

Materials

- Chromebooks
- Google Maps
- Google Suite
- Library databases
- Other online resources

Lesson

Before: Learners begin this lesson having already learned about the Reconstruction era in U.S. history with their classroom educator. Learners know that they are expected to connect prior knowledge in order to discover how well the promises made during Reconstruction were or were not kept.

During: Learners work both individually and with their team to learn about the key events, people, and legislation of the civil rights movement. Concepts are introduced by the educator partner in the classroom and then learners visit the school library to interact in stations with books and online resources to discover, understand, and apply knowledge. Learners move through these stations or modules and conclude each station or module with a whole-group share-out.

Assessment: Assess the learner teams' Google Doc for understanding of the content and equity in each member's contributions. Assess each learner independently on the ability to apply the content learned to a civil rights–based Advanced Placement long essay question. Assess learners on how well they used materials and on their annotated bibliography. Have learners use a checklist to self-assess their mastery of the content and their contributions to the team.

The art of teaching is the art of assisting discovery.

—Mark van Doren

Conclusion: Digesting Inquire

The magic that is involved in preparing a meal is what makes a chef famous. How that individual adds to a foundation of protein, vegetable, and starch using spices and cooking techniques is what makes the chef renowned. Inquiry is much like being a chef; it is the process of bringing questions and resources together to create new learning—the chef's masterpiece. School librarians and their educator partners are the facilitators, sous-chefs if you will, who allow learners to create their masterpieces through engaging in an inquiry process, stirring in the Shared Foundation of Inquire with core content.

Inquire as a Culinary Science

Throughout this book, the Shared Foundation of Inquire focuses on inspiring learners' curiosity and initiative during an inquiry unit and on how school librarians and other educators can help support this curiosity and initiative by creating opportunities for engagement. Engaging the learner from the beginning of the unit is crucial for building the dispositions for continually seeking knowledge and engaging in sustained inquiry so that learners can share products with an authentic audience. Several key ingredients are important to keep in mind as you mix and match the flavors of inquiry and facilitate your learners as head chefs in their own inquiry learning.

QUESTIONING

The first Competency of Inquire asks learners to formulate questions. In fact, all inquiry process models begin with questioning. Questioning is the basis of the definition of *inquire*— "to ask about; to search into." Teaching learners how to ask good questions and how to use those questions to find answers in quality resources takes time. Developing a culture of inquiry in which questions are accepted and often asked builds learners' capacity for knowing what a good question is and what it is not. Learners also begin to see that the types of questions asked will bring about certain types of answers or nonanswers. When used with inquiry process models, questioning protocols teach learners good questioning skills that become part of any content that learners are learning.

CRITICAL THINKING

Studies have shown that learners need to be able to employ critical-thinking skills so that they can work with others to solve problems in a workforce that hasn't been created yet. The skills of critical and creative thinking, as well as the abilities to collaborate and communicate with others, can be enhanced through learning content and developing information literacy skills. In planning and delivering inquiry units, school librarians and their educator partners need to scaffold lessons and learning so that learners are comfortable performing these skills. Process models walk the learner through stages that scaffold learning so that the learner can move through an inquiry unit from start to finish with some feeling of success.

REAL-WORLD CONNECTIONS

By connecting content learning to the real world or simulating real-world applications, school librarians and educator partners help learners see value in the learning process and thereby become engaged with the learning. Developing inquiry units with learners that involve some sort of service learning or community help beyond themselves encourages learners to become empathetic citizens who see value in making their community a better place for everyone.

VOICE AND CHOICE

Allowing learners to have some ownership in their learning process inspires curiosity and initiative. Ownership equals engagement. Voice and choice within the framework of the inquiry unit can be scaffolded for the age and ability levels of learners. Not only does allowing voice and choice create deeper engagement with the content, but learners are also more likely to retain the content and skills and produce products worth sharing with an authentic audience. Allowing voice and choice is one of the best ways to engage learners and build the disposition to continue. Be cautious, though, in how much voice and choice is given in any learning unit. Too much, and learners could struggle without the guidance that scaffolding lessons can provide. Too little voice and choice stifles the engagement factor and the interest to see the learning through to completion. All inquiry process models have scaffolds built into them, allowing school librarians and educator partners to become the guide on the side.

TRANSFERABLE SKILLS

No matter the course content, all learning units can be planned so that the content engages learners to want to understand and do more for themselves, building convergent, divergent, and metacognitive thinking skills. When learners find success through the inquiry process, they are more likely to take that success to the next inquiry learning experience, even if that learning is in a different subject area.

NONLINEAR LEARNING

When designing inquiry research units, it is important to remember that learners need time to devise and implement plans to fill knowledge gaps. Learners need to understand that the inquiry process is nonlinear. The AASL Standards and all inquiry process models note that they are nonlinear. Learners may have to move forward and backward in order to get to the end of the process and be able to demonstrate learning. These nonlinear methods also help learners build the disposition to persevere and find some level of success.

REFLECTION

The last theme stressed through the Shared Foundation of Inquire and the inquiry process models explored is reflection. Reflection is not just for school librarians and their educator partners. It also shouldn't be done only at the end of the unit. Learners need to reflect on the process and the product. Learners also need to learn how to be respectful and constructive when giving and receiving feedback with their peers. Reflection helps learners with developing skills to manage their learning, develop the disposition to persevere, and learn how they themselves learn. School librarians and other educators need to be reflective during the inquiry unit as well. This reflection can be done formally or informally with assessments and scaffolded lessons throughout the learning.

Blending the Shared Foundations

The *National School Library Standards for Learners, School Librarians, and School Libraries* are purposeful in presenting the Shared Foundation of Inquire first among the frameworks because many learning experiences begin with inquiry. But just as the Competencies and Alignments for learners, school librarians, and school libraries are interdependent, no "Shared Foundation can be effectively executed independent of the [others]" (AASL 2018, 17) (see figure C.1). The elements in Inquire's Key Commitment to "build new knowledge by inquiring, thinking critically, identifying problems, and developing strategies for solving problems" (AASL 2018, 70) are part of the base for any unit recipe featuring one or more of the six Shared Foundations—Inquire, Include, Collaborate, Curate, Explore, and Engage.

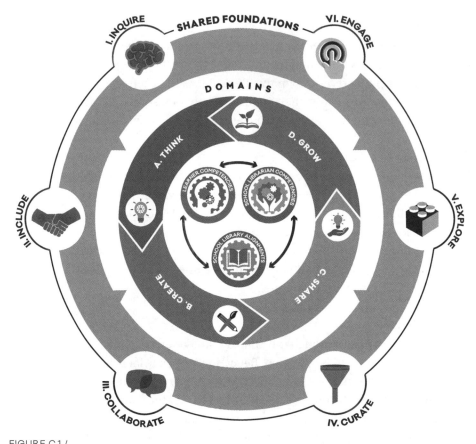

FIGURE C.1 /
Integrated Framework Wheel

A wheel chart illustrating the relationship of the components within the AASL Standards framework structure.

THINK

When learners formulate questions and use their prior knowledge as a context for new meaning, they "[adopt] a discerning stance toward points of view and opinions expressed in information resources and learning products" (AASL 2018, Learner II.A.2.). From these points of view, learners then can "[demonstrate] their desire to broaden and deepen understandings" related to their new knowledge by "making critical choices about information sources to use" (AASL 2018, Learner III.A.1., IV.A.3.). As learners work through the inquiry process, they are "reading widely and deeply in multiple formats and writ[ing] and creat[ing] for a variety of purposes" all the while "evaluating information for accuracy, validity, social and cultural context, and appropriateness for need" (AASL 2018, Learner V.A.1., VI.A.3.).

CREATE

When the research part of the inquiry unit is completed, learners have an opportunity to fill knowledge gaps so that a product that demonstrates their learning can be created. During this time learners will have "[evaluated] a variety of perspectives during learning activities" to understand differing perspectives and rule out biases (AASL 2018, Learner II.B.2.). Learners use "a variety of communication tools and resources" to plan creation of their final products as well as learn how to "systematically [question] and [assess] the validity and accuracy of information" through mini-lessons provided by the school librarian (AASL 2018, Learner III.B.1., IV.B.3.). As learners work through creating their final products, they problem solve "through cycles of design, implementation, and reflection" while "acknowledging authorship and demonstrating respect for the intellectual property of others" (AASL 2018, Learner V.B.1., VI.B.2.).

SHARE

As the inquiry unit winds down, learners are now ready to share their new knowledge as they adapt, communicate, and exchange learning products for peer review, for conferencing with the school librarian and collaborating educator, or for both. Learners are taught how to give and receive constructive feedback by "contributing to discussions in which multiple viewpoints on a topic are expressed" and by "soliciting and responding to feedback from others" (AASL 2018, Learner II.C.2., III.C.1.). After "accessing and evaluating collaboratively constructed information sites," and "expressing curiosity about a topic of personal interest or curricular relevance," learners are ready to create and share their final products (AASL 2018, Learner IV.C.1., V.C.1.). School librarians can work with learners during this part of the inquiry unit with lessons on "sharing information resources in accordance with modification, reuse, and remix policies" (AASL 2018, Learner VI.C.1.).

GROW

Throughout the unit, the school librarian and collaborating educator have designed ways to help learners continually seek knowledge throughout the inquiry process and allow for reflection along the way. During this time, it is also important for learners to "[seek] interactions with a range of [other] learners," helping learners see gaps in knowledge gathering and learn from a variety of perspectives (AASL 2018, Learner II.D.1.). When learners have an opportunity to work with others, they build communication skills by "actively contributing to group discussions" and "recognizing learning as a social responsibility" (AASL 2018, Learner III.D.1., III.D.2.). By "openly communicating curation processes for others to use, interpret, and validate," learners share and grow new knowledge (AASL 2018, Learner IV.D.3.). Learners also advance their social and emotional development through this feedback process by "open-mindedly accepting feedback for positive and constructive growth" and "reflecting on the process of ethical generation of knowledge" (AASL 2018, Learner V.D.3., VI.D.2.).

•••

Through the Shared Foundation of Inquire, learners learn to ask questions, think critically, identify problems, and develop strategies for solving problems while stretching into the other Shared Foundations supporting their growth and competency development. In tandem, these Shared Foundations can be applied at any point of entry, at any grade level, at any skill level, and with any content area. How exciting it is to see how Inquire is infused throughout the Shared Foundations and how the Shared Foundations infuse each other when planning, facilitating, and working through inquiry units with learners and other educators! I hope this examination of Inquire has inspired your own curiosity and initiative as you move forward, cultivating mindsets and cultures in your community!

Works Cited

AASL American Association of School Librarians. 2018. *National School Library Standards for Learners, School Librarians, and School Libraries.* Chicago: ALA Editions, an imprint of the American Library Association.

AASL American Association of School Librarians. 2019. "Role of the School Library." www.ala.org/aasl/sites/ala.org.aasl/files/content/advocacy/statements/docs/AASL_Role_of_the_School_Library.pdf.

AASL American Association of School Librarians. Forthcoming. "Instructional Role of the School Librarian."

AI Commons. n.d.a. "5 Classic Principles of AI." https://appreciativeinquiry.champlain.edu/learn/appreciative-inquiry-introduction/5-classic-principles-ai.

AI Commons. n.d.b. "Introduction to Appreciative Inquiry." https://appreciativeinquiry.champlain.edu/learn/appreciative-inquiry-introduction.

Benson, Theresa. n.d. "Plan, Do, Review . . . What's Bugging You? (Grades PreK–2): An Information Literacy Lesson Plan for Young Children." Big6 Lessons. https://static1.squarespace.com/static/59a303936a49631dd51f9a7d/t/5b9e7eb30e2e72b096914ac1/1537113780249/PlanDoReviewBuggingYou.pdf.

Berger, Warren. 2016. *A More Beautiful Question: The Power of Inquiry to Spark Breakthrough Ideas.* Paperback ed. New York: Bloomsbury.

Berkowitz, Robert E. n.d. "U.S. History, Civil War: A Study in Change." Big6 Lessons. https://static1.squarespace.com/static/59a303936a49631dd51f9a7d/t/5b9e877a032be486708f64c4/1537116026764/Civil+War.pdf.

Big6. n.d. "Big6 Skills Overview." The Big6: Information and Technology Skills for Student Success. https://static1.squarespace.com/static/59a303936a49631dd51f9a7d/t/5b92bf5e03ce644e10c18005/1536343902416/Big6+Skills+Overview.pdf.

Callison, Daniel, and Katie Baker. 2014. "Elements of Information Inquiry, Evolution of Models, and Measured Reflection." *Knowledge Quest* 43 (2): 18–24.

Couros, George. 2015. *The Innovator's Mindset: Empower Learning, Unleash Talent, and Lead a Culture of Creativity.* San Diego, CA: Dave Burgess Consulting.

"Create a Question Formulation Technique Lesson Plan with This Online Tool." 2017. Right Question Institute. http://rightquestion.org/blog/create-a-question-formulation-technique-lesson-plan-with-this-online-tool.

Eisenberg, Michael B., and Robert E. Berkowitz. 2000. *Teaching Information and Technology Skills: The Big6 in Secondary Schools.* Worthington, OH: Linworth.

Eisenberg, Mike, and Bob Berkowitz. 2014, January. *Inquiry Learning Big6-Style: It All Starts with Asking Great Questions!* Webinar.

Facing History and Ourselves. 2018. "Analyzing Nazi Propaganda." Holocaust and Human Behavior. https://www.facinghistory.org/holocaust-and-human-behavior/analyzing-nazi-propaganda.

"Gallery Walk." n.d. The Teacher Toolkit. http://www.theteachertoolkit.com/index.php/tool/gallery-walk.

Glossary of Education Reform. 2013. "Growth Mindset." https://www.edglossary.org/growth-mindset/.

Harada, Violet H., and Joan M. Yoshina. 2010. *Assessing for Learning: Librarians and Teachers as Partners.* 2nd ed. Santa Barbara, CA: Libraries Unlimited.

Harvard Project Zero. n.d.a. "See Think Wonder: A Routine for Exploring Works of Art and Other Interesting Things." Visible Thinking. http://www.visiblethinkingpz.org/VisibleThinking_html_files/03_ThinkingRoutines/03c_Core_routines/SeeThinkWonder/SeeThinkWonder_Routine.html.

———. n.d.b. "Thinking Routines." Visible Thinking. http://www.visiblethinkingpz.org/VisibleThinking_html_files/VisibleThinking1.html.

Heick, Terry. 2017. "4 Phases of Inquiry-Based Learning: A Guide for Teachers." TeachThought. https://www.teachthought.com/pedagogy/4-phases-inquiry-based-learning-guide-teachers/.

Holland, Beth. 2017. "Inquiry and the Research Process." *Edutopia* (blog). October 26. https://www.edutopia.org/article/inquiry-and-research-process.

"How Might We" Questions. 2019. Hasso Plattner Institute of Design at Stanford University. https://dschool-staging.squarespace.com/resources/how-might-we-questions.

Hutcherson, Trisha. 2017. "Americans Who Made a Difference: Popplets, Paper People, and Videos!" *52 Weeks of Guided Inquiry* (blog). March 10. https://52guidedinquiry.edublogs.org/2017/03/10/americans-who-made-a-difference-popplets-paper-people-and-videos.

Jansen, Barbara. 2004. *Evaluating Big6 Units.* https://static1.squarespace.com/static/59a303936a49631dd51f9a7d/t/5b92e2e54d7a9cece563a55b/1536352997816/Evaluating_Big6_Units.pdf.

Kagan, Spencer, and Miguel Kagan. 2015. *Kagan Cooperative Learning.* San Clemente, CA: Kagan Publishing.

Kuhlthau, Carol Collier, Leslie K. Maniotes, and Ann K. Caspari. 2012. *Guided Inquiry Design: A Framework for Inquiry in Your School.* Santa Barbara, CA: Libraries Unlimited.

———. 2015. *Guided Inquiry: Learning in the 21st Century.* 2nd ed. Santa Barbara, CA: ABC-Clio.

Lloyd, Carol. 2015. "5 Ideas for Promoting Student-Generated Questions." *Thinking Maps* (blog). March 9. https://www.thinkingmaps.com/5-strategies-promoting-student-generated-questions.

Loertscher, David V., Carol Koechlin, and Sandi Zwaan. 2005. *Ban Those Bird Units! 15 Models for Teaching and Learning in Information-Rich and Technology-Rich Environments.* Salt Lake City, UT: Hi Willow.

McCarthy, John. 2016. "Need to Know Process for PBL and Quality Units." *Opening Paths: Creating Solutions to Empower Learners* (blog). June 16. http://openingpaths.org/blog/2015/02/need-to-know-process/.

Minigan, Andrew, Sarah Westbrook, Dan Rothstein, and Luz Santana. 2017. "Stimulating and Sustaining Inquiry with Students' Questions." http://rightquestion.org/wp-content/uploads/2012/04/Right-Question-Institute-Stimulating-and-sustaining-inquiry-with-students-questions.pdf.

MyPBLWorks. n.d. "Projects." Buck Institute for Education. https://my.pblworks.org/projects.

NEA National Education Association. 2017. "K-W-L (Know, Want to Know, Learned)." NEA: Tools and Ideas. http://www.nea.org/tools/k-w-l-know-want-to-know-learned.html.

Neebe, Diana, and Jen Roberts. 2015. *Power Up: Making the Shift to 1:1 Teaching and Learning.* Portland, ME: Stenhouse Publishers.

Pappas, Marjorie L., and Ann E. Tepe. 2002. *Pathways to Knowledge and Inquiry Learning.* Greenwood Village, CO: Libraries Unlimited.

PBLWorks. n.d. "What Is PBL?" Buck Institute for Education. https://www.pblworks.org/what-is-pbl.

ReadWriteThink. 2019. "K-W-L Chart." ILA/NCTE. http://www.readwritethink.org/classroom-resources/printouts/chart-a-30226.html.

Ritchhart, Ron, Mark Church, and Karin Morrison. 2011. *Making Thinking Visible: How to Promote Engagement, Understanding, and Independence for All Learners.* San Francisco, CA: Jossey-Bass.

Rothstein, Dan, and Luz Santana. 2011. *Make Just One Change: Teach Students to Ask Their Own Questions*. Cambridge, MA: Harvard Education Press.

RQI Right Question Institute. 2018. "Teach Students to Ask Their Own Questions." *Classroom Practice* (blog). http://rightquestion.org/education.

School Reform Initiative. n.d. *The 5 Whys for Inquiry of Group Questions*. https://www.schoolreforminitiative.org/download/the-5-whys-for-inquiry -of-group-questions/.

Schwartz, Katrina. 2017. "Developing Students' Ability to Give and Take Effective Feedback." *MindShift* (blog). October 15. https://www.kqed.org/mindshift/ 49243/developing-students-ability-to-give-and-take-effective-feedback.

Simkins, Michael, Karen Cole, Fern Tavalin, and Barbara Means. 2002. "Making a Real-World Connection." Chap. 3 in *Increasing Student Learning through Multimedia Projects*. Alexandria, VA: ASCD. http://www.ascd.org/publications/ books/102112/chapters/Making_a_Real-World_Connection.aspx.

Steere, Luke. 2018. "Tripping Over Poetry." *52 Weeks of Guided Inquiry* (blog). June 20. http://52guidedinquiry.edublogs.org/2018/06/20.

Stripling, Barbara K. 2003. "Inquiry-Based Learning." In *Curriculum Connections through the Library*, by Barbara K. Stripling and Sandra Hughes-Hassell, 3–31. Principles and Practice. Westport, CT: Libraries Unlimited.

Tan, Zhai Yun. 2016. "OK, Google, Where Did I Put My Thinking Cap?" NPR: *All Tech Considered.* February 5. https://www.npr.org/sections/alltechconsidered/ 2016/02/05/465699380/ok-google-where-did-i-put-my-thinking-cap.

TeachThought Staff. 2018. "5 Strategies for Incorporating Social Emotional Learning into Your Classroom." https://www.teachthought.com/pedagogy/5-strategies -for-incorporating-social-emotional-learning-into-your-classroom.

Watanabe-Crockett, Lee. 2017. "A List of Over 100 Awesome Essential Questions Examples by Subject." Global Digital Citizenship Foundation. https://global digitalcitizen.org/100-awesome-essential-questions.

"What Are Thinking Maps?" n.d. Thinking Maps. https://www.thinkingmaps.com/ why-thinking-maps-2.

Whitney, Diana Kaplin, and Amanda Trosten-Bloom. 2010. *The Power of Appreciative Inquiry: A Practical Guide to Positive Change*. 2nd ed. San Francisco: Berrett-Koehler.

Wiggins, Grant, and Jay McTighe. 2005. *Understanding by Design*. Expanded 2nd ed. Alexandria, VA: ASCD.

About the Author

LORI DONOVAN is a National Board Certified Librarian and is the K–12 library services specialist for Chesterfield County (Virginia) Public Schools. She holds a master's degree in education with a specialty in school librarianship and a graduate professional endorsement in educational leadership from Longwood University. She has published several articles in *Library Media Connection,* is a columnist for *School Library Connection,* and has coauthored *Power Researchers: Transforming Student Library Aides into Action Learners* (Libraries Unlimited). Lori has served on many AASL committees and has held several elected offices. She is also a past president of the Virginia Association of School Librarians.

Contributors

Shelley Armstrong, Chesterfield County Public Schools, Virginia
Robbie Barber, DeKalb County School District, Georgia
Laurie Bolt, Newport News Public Schools, Virginia
Susanna Carey, Fairfax County Public Schools, Virginia
Jennifer Cooper, Prince William County Public Schools, Virginia
Brandon Filsinger, Fairfax County Public Schools, Virginia
Diana Garbera, Chesterfield County Public Schools, Virginia
Debi Graves, Chesterfield County Public Schools, Virginia
Gretchen Hazlin, Fairfax County Public Schools, Virginia
Heather Hess, Wallenpaupack Area School District, Pennsylvania
Lara Ivey, Chesterfield County Public Schools, Virginia
Brooksie Kramer, Campbell County Schools Public Schools, Virginia
Patty Lambusta, Newport News Public Schools, Virginia
Emily Mazzanti, Chesterfield County Public Schools, Virginia
Daniel McCulley, Chesterfield County Public Schools, Virginia
Carolyn Moul, Chesterfield County Public Schools, Virginia
Heather Murfee, Chesterfield County Public Schools, Virginia
Pam Rockenbach, Chesterfield County Public Schools, Virginia
Caroline Romano, Wallenpaupack Area School District, Pennsylvania
Rita Saylor, Wallenpaupack Area School District, Pennsylvania
Sue Strada, Wallenpaupack Area School District, Pennsylvania
Marie Taloute, Newport News Public Schools, Virginia
Julie Trammell-McGill, Albemarle County Public Schools, Virginia
Leslie Vaughn, Chesterfield County Public Schools, Virginia
Carolyn Vibbert, Prince William County Public Schools, Virginia
Donald Walutes, Wallenpaupack Area School District, Pennsylvania

Index

An italicized page number indicates an illustration or table.

assessment of learners
    formative, 37–38, 39, 40, 61, 62, 83, 107–111,
        114–115, 116, 121, 151, 152
    by peers, 29, 36, 40, 45, 107–111, 165, 167
    self-reflection. *See* reflection, by learners
        (fostered by educators)
    summative, 114–115
    See also lesson examples
Austin's Butterfly, 109, 159
authentic audience, 29, 80, 83, 84, 85, 107–111,
    163, 164
    See also inquiry process models; lesson
        examples
Ayoa task management tool, 62

B

Backchannel Chat, 61
banned books lesson, 70–71
Barber, Robbie, 69–70
Basecamp, 151
Becoming an Author lesson, 125–126
benefits
    of Appreciative Inquiry, 22–24, 30–31
    of blending Shared Foundations, 165–168
    Inquiry culture, xvii, 45, 51, 163–164
    of inquiry in learning, 3–8, 35
Berger, Ron, 109
Berger, Warren, 3, 4, 16, 23
Berkowitz, Bob, 10
Big6 model infographic, *12*
Big6 model of inquiry
    in context of all AASL Standards Domains,
        10–11, *12*
    in context of Create Domain, *28*, 76–77, 78–79,
        84
    in context of Grow Domain, 30, 136
    in context of Share Domain, *29*, 108, 114, 115
    in context of Think Domain, *27*, 45, 52–53
biography lesson, 100
Blackboard learning management system, 66–69
Blogger, 123
blogging, 122–123
board game creation lesson, 128–130
Bolt, Laurie, 128–130, 158–159
Book Creator, 95, 123, 126
book writing lesson, 125–126
Boolean logic lesson, 69–70
Boomwriter, 95, 123, 126, 151
Borreguita and the Coyote: A Tale from Ayutla,
    Mexico, 157–158
brain research in the context of learning, 22
brainstorming, 18, 47, 53, 58–59, 63, 77, 122, 160
Buck Institute for Education, 17
Buffer, 151
Buncee tool, 124

C

Canva online design tool, 94
Canvas learning management system, 66–69
career readiness, 54, 113, 114, 142, 148, 151
Carey, Susanna, 101–102
Carle, Eric, 52
Caspari, Ann K., 10
cause and effect, 18–19, 150, 161–162
Chalk Talk thinking routine, 59
challenge thinking, 110
choice and voice for learners. *See* voice and
    choice for learners
choice questions in Guided Inquiry Design, 76
Circle of Viewpoints protocol, 122
citing sources, 63, 64–65, 67, 70–71, 103, 108, 109,
    131, 151
civil rights movement lesson, 161–162
Civil War and Reconstruction lesson, 53
Civil War Biographies lesson, 100
Civil War lesson, 68–69
Claim-Support-Question thinking routine, 60
classbuilding concept, 36, 110, 124
ClassHook website, 61
cognitive domain of learning. *See* Think Domain
    in Inquire Shared Foundation
Collaborate Shared Foundation competencies
    for learners, 166–167
collaboration
    among educators, 8, 20, 22, 24–25, 31, 37, 40,
        46, 49, 57, 80, 83–86, 119, 142, 164. *See*
        also lesson examples
    among learners, 44–45, 47, 51–53, 83, 89,
        121–124, 141
    in context of 4 Cs, 93, 113. *See also* lesson
        examples
    importance of, 39, 121, 135, 140, 142, 146, 165
    methods for fostering in learners, 5, 10, 35, 38,
        39, 43, 44, 51–52, 59, 62, 81, 84, 87–90, 95,
        107, 113, 114, 121–124, 146, 151
Collaborize Classroom, 61
collection development, 87–89
college readiness, 113, 142
Common Sense Media website, 108
communication skills
    in context of 4 Cs, 44, 93, 113
    fostering in learners, 12–13, *14*, *30*, 47, 53, 54,
        62, 79, 84, 88, 91, 107, 109, 114, 123, 140,
        142, 150, 164, 167
    importance of, 140
    See also lesson examples
community readiness. *See* life readiness
Compass Points routine, 122
competencies for learners
    Collaborate Shared Foundation, 166–167
    Curate Shared Foundation, 166–167